MOURNING WHISKERS

MOURNING WHISKERS

KATHRYN SCHWAUSCH BRANSON

ISBN: 979-8-89228-592-6   (Paperback)
ISBN: 979-8-89228-593-3   (Hardcover)
ISBN: 979-8-89228-594-0   (eBook)

Printed in the United States of America

Acknowledgements

by *Kathryn Schwausch Branson*

To My Cousin, Marylin Jean Hoblet

I lovingly include my very fabulous, gutsy, forthright, delicate, blue-eyed, gentle, and sweet cousin, **Marylin Jean Hoblet**. She is my fellow cohort in careers — "white dresses, white hats, white shoes" — as we both chose nursing for our life's work.

We even worked hand in hand, choosing affiliated specialties associated with surgical nursing. Marylin worked in both pre-op and post-op surgical areas, while I began in labor and delivery. After leaving Texas for Chattanooga, I found myself drawn to intensive care units, which inspired me to attend Nurse Anesthesia School.

Perhaps it was because I wanted to focus on just one patient. As Marylin will agree, nurses need three hands, eyes in the back of their heads, and the quirky ability to read both the surgeon's and anesthesiologist's minds. Over the years, I believe we acquired those essential skills!

Eventually, we disrobed our starched white dresses and pristine hats to don freshly washed scrubs every day—sometimes several times a day. We love telling stories from our days at work, stories that TV shows could never capture, and which remain our sacred memories as nurses.

Childhood Memories with Marylin

Growing up, my brother Russell and I were always thrilled when our parents said we were going to visit our cousins in Giddings. The air was crystal clear and cool, and the dirt beneath our feet was red.

We were fascinated by the variety of animals Uncle Gus and Aunt Ella kept on their farm—especially their ducks and geese who greeted us loudly. Aunt Ella even had her own Brahma bull named *Bingo*, while our bull at home was *Domino*!

Our family gatherings were filled with laughter, games of 42, dominoes, and cards. The tension of competition was always lightened by our Wendish/German heritage—aluminum tubs filled with ice-cold beer for the adults, and soda water in glass bottles for the children.

The best part of those visits was exploring the ponds (or "tanks," as we called them) and skipping rocks across the water. I was mesmerized by the cattails growing along the banks, a memory that remains vivid to this day.

It's no wonder my home in Tennessee is beside the North Chickamauga Creek—where, much to my neighbors' dismay, I planted bamboo to prevent erosion. It worked for a while… until it grew through their decks! Oops. ☺

A Family Legacy of Faith

On one visit, Uncle Gus and my father, Hermann, had a serious conversation with my fifteen-year-old son, Austin. They told him they believed he had the qualities of a Biblically sound pastor. Today, Austin is an ordained pastor with a loving congregation who, as I like to say, "will never give him back to me."

Moments like that remind me that mothers have mysterious influence. We're often blamed for everything, but I choose to believe that good clings to the bad, like a magnet throughout our children's lives.

My father was a farmer and a creative carpenter, often scavenging from junkyards to create masterpieces. One famous story involves little Marylin climbing to the top of a tall slide. Her father, Uncle Gus, rescued her just in time, and they slid down together safely. "All's well that ends well!"

Marylin and I often share deep spiritual conversations, strengthened by the devout Christian teachings of her parents—a reminder that **Jesus is alive.**

God bless you, Marylin Jean.

To My Cousin, Elaine Ruth Schlomach

It is most significant to include **Elaine Ruth Schlomach** in my acknowledgements. Elaine has taken on much responsibility—she is the *Queen Bee* of our tribe! Whenever anything happens in our family, Elaine is the first to know, and the one who keeps us all connected.

She is the needle and thread that binds us together, preserving our traditions that began long ago in Texas when our ancestors—Wends from Prussia—settled to farm and worship freely. Church was the center of our community: Sunday services, weddings, picnics, and school events. Every birthday was celebrated without exception.

Elaine's expertise in baking wedding cakes is legendary; once word got out, she never said no! Her heart is filled with care for everyone she meets. Truly, she is our *Wendish Encyclopedia.*

Her parents, Arthur Robert Mathis Schwausch and Ruth Anna Gertrude Schwausch, were affectionately nicknamed "ARMS" and "RAGS" by their initials. Aunt Ruth was anything but rags—she was pure silk and gold, full of kindness and devotion. Elaine has continued that legacy beautifully.

When I was in Vanderbilt Hospital after back surgeries, Elaine sent me a handmade Christmas ornament in the shape of a cross, reminding me to keep one special decoration up all year as a symbol of our faith.

Elaine, I believe God threw away the mold after making you. The world only deserved **one authentic Elaine Ruth.**

We all love you.

To My Niece, Robin Mierzejewski (Robbibobbin)

A very special person in my life is my first niece, **Robin Mierzejewski**, whom I affectionately call *Robbibobbin*. Her letters from college first inspired me to value the power of written words.

Our shared roots in Texas are deep, and we've always shared a fascination with birds—especially peacocks and roadrunners. Peacocks, symbols of immortality, remind me of my father's cherished pets, whose feathers I still keep on display.

The roadrunner, or *chaparral*, symbolizes good luck and protection. For us, seeing one feels like a visit from our fathers—messages from Heaven in swift motion.

Robin has an exceptional gift for expressing emotion through words, weaving beauty from letters like a bouquet of meaning.

To my dear Robbibobbin,
the light from your golden eyes shines a steady, brilliant ray of hope in my life—from Texas all the way to Tennessee.

You are truly most dear.
My love I send to you, heartfelt and sincere. 🖤🐾🖤
Your one and only Aunt Kat Feet — who will have you for eternity to keep.

To My Atticus Publishing Family

I wish to acknowledge my Production Specialist and dear friend, **Daisy Brown**, of Atticus Book Publishing. Daisy has been attentive to all of my concerns and has encouraged my artistic style, even asking to use a section of my *Grand Canyon Mural* as her cell phone wallpaper—an incredible honor!

Her melodic, friendly voice always lifts my spirits. Daisy is a charming yet powerful force who believes in me and motivates me to fulfill my writing and art dreams.

Thank you, Daisy. 🌼

To My Editor, Tina Summers

My deepest gratitude also goes to **Tina Summers**, my editor. From the first time I heard her voice, I knew she was a kindred spirit. We both experienced near-death experiences, yet God kept us here for His divine purpose.

Tina has written two heartfelt poems for me, which I keep in my "Tina Journal" to reread when I need comfort and encouragement. Her story of survival and strength, and her unwavering dedication to her family, inspire me deeply.

Tina, you brighten the world. ✺

To My 4 Grandsons and my 1 Granddaughter

Lastly, I dedicate this book to my grandkids, who have proven themselves to be the strongest and most courageous young kids I know.

May God continue to hold their hands, guide them through life's challenges, and lead them to fulfilling, adventurous lives—always safe in the loving arms of Jesus.

God is good. 🕆

Kathryn Schwausch Branson
June 23, 2025

Table of Contents

FROM THE TIME OF OUR BIRTH

Onto this Earth
It might be apropos to suppose
We have entered a World with Those
Who have timely joined our beginning
Of MOURNING
Which besets
Our very element
OF LIFE

Taking into account every cell
And all our finely, nigh-to-invisible
Filaments, that are attempting to
Fool MOTHER NATURE.

Although SHE is never confused about
Our Google, GPS, and conflicting
Road MAPS,
MOTHER NATURE is precise in reaching
OUR DESTINATION
STATION.

The main question then for us is
Whether our landing sits
On our RIGHT or on the LEFT,
WIDE, EXPANSIVE CLEFT.

We look around and notice herds of
SHEEP on one side and even larger
Herds of GOATS on the other.
Strange it seems; we mutter.

We were expecting angels and a
SYMPHONY of MESMERIZING
Voices singing HALLELUJAH
In a key and TONE
We had never KNOWN.

But what do you think about being
Introduced to masses of loud, cloven-
Hoofed ruminant mammals?

Not a single SOUL or beast wearing
WOVEN matching pairs of
Shoes or GLORIOUS CROWNS
Presenting themselves RENOWNED!

The best way to celebrate LIFE
Is to get in touch with MOURNING.
Everything that was before us has
PASSED; however, when danger comes
And death edges closely by us,
Scratching our skin cells,
A FLOCK OF ANGELS
CIRCLE ABOUT US,
LOCKING WINGS,
NOT LETTING
DEATH
IN.

Millions of shutter-rate views
Attack our eyes, as if this will
Help us here in the NOW.
The devil is consummatory in
Juggling with time.
The way he operates and conquers is
Through patience with his half-baked
Devices and lies.

We notice another SATANIC MOVE
As he grinds on our heels,
Holding us down and,
Believe me, brother,
He will not relent.
He is hell-bent.

The ONLY way out is to seek GOD.
That millisecond we knew,
It's so simple and easy,
Making it exceptionally difficult to do.

As a CHILD we could reach GOD in a precise moment of
thought,
Using PRAYERS LINING the walls of our
CLEAN MINDS,
Tucked neatly with
No stuttering, stalling, speed bumps, or
SIGNS.

Our call to THE LORD darting out
Through slick passages connecting
Our uncluttered FAITH, delivered to HEAVEN IN A
STREAMLINED, fast pace.

All happening faster than the speed of light or the sound of a
boom.
Instantaneously GOD LIFTS US UP,
Carrying us away from our precarious
DOOM.

And when HE sets us back down,
We see WHITE FEATHERS and red smears
Streaking every which way, covering the
GROUND. We are once again SAFE and
SOUND. ✝

This wasn't our first close call, and as
WE AGE, we know it's not our last,
Not until GOD places us on the
Bottom rung of HIS LADDER.
We climb, not seeing the top step;
The further we go upward, the lighter
We tap.
THEN KNOWING FULLY GOD IS TAKING
US BACK.

ONCE WE ARE HIGH ABOVE ANYONE'S
SIGHT,
THIS IS THE TIME for the people
BELOW us to start MOURNING OUR LIVES.

WE REFLECT DOWN TO THEM,

OUR SACRED HALLELUJAH
LIGHT. ☀

Thus the time we are born
Until the time we cease,
OUR minimum time above ground,
We are in a constant state of grief.

This is or should be, so obviously true,
Because we all know early in life
Death is, most certainly,
Where we're headed,
Our daily strife.

There are no U-turns or off-ramps,
So each day that we finish, we can
MOURN without tears and REJOICE,
As it takes us closer to our MAKER
ABOVE; all choices are finalized.

We live without perplexion within
Bodies PERFECTED, HOME TO A
PRIME TIME OF OUR LIFE,
AS WE WORSHIP GOD,
EVERLASTING,
ETERNAL,
YOUTH.

Kathryn SchwauSch Branson
4-22-2025

BEACHED BOTTLE

NOT going to bed at midnight
NOT getting up at ten A.M.
Reason being having
Chest pain tonight

Actually, it is now morning, and
My chest has left and flew
The second you told me
What I was going to do

That was the instant, moment
Panic hit, gagging my squeak.
STOP telling me I'm NOT to talk,
It took me two decades to speak.

Now that I've begun, no one
Wants to hear a hushed bleep.
Once I stop, I may never relearn;
Then my friends could sigh a relief.

You only want to reshape me,
That window of time has closed.
I'd rather you take me where I'm in,
Because my life is no place you've been.

Would take ninety-nine years to get the jest
Of being who you have in mind I am.
Ease OFF, Ease OFF, Ease OFF; best
Let's start fresh all over, iffen we can.

I appreciate your advice,
Stabs into my ribs like a knife.
All I hear is you do not accept me;
Must be dismantled, get reassemble key.

Probably a no-go, as my life is nigh to
Over; just leave me to fade out this way.
You receive me excited, overly passionate;
You think it is your duty to arrange me laze.

After a bout with you I slump into
Silence and misery for a run of days.
Shut-down, Shut-out, nowhere near
Anyone to be calm, no fuss, just quiet craze.

The answer has come to me, I'll disappear.
Slide me into bottle with note written hush;
Over-talking snuck in, jarred my mind mush.
Replace me back into my past empty bottle.

Row me way out of sight to sea, flipping
Me over with letters enclosed and folded.
I'll delay into whisper your wish to stop me
From voicing anything, my lips glued sealed.

Kathryn SchwauSch Branson
5-17- 2025

BOWING IN FULL ARRAY

Mother Nature is true to herself as she is,

Nurtured and clothed in Glory.

Everything in this world outside of people

Is harmonious, in perfect ORDER.

We have much to learn from this woman:

MOTHER NATURE.

Free will made us think we could chase her.

We thought we were cool enough to win.

Truth is, we will never catch up or come

Close enough to touch her hem.

Even so, she returns gracefully, bowing in

Full array to greet us each and every day.

This alone gives us a reason to live, to be

With her, to keep on trying, and to give,

As we have bountifully received so much.

Maybe we may learn her way; get in touch.

What a transformation when we ourselves

Greet Mother Nature in full array, giving too,

Back to Earth what we've received, waking

Up in splendid full array, greeting

Mother Nature; bidding her a

Naturally glorious,

Wondrous day.

Thanking GOD, WHO

We bow to and bestow

ALL PRAISE.

Kathryn SchwauSch Branson
7-24-2025

BURIED STEAK

When almost a year elapsed without
Social contact, gatherings, or over-nighters,
My Grandson's dad allowed his youngest
A trip for a pajama party at Grandma's nest.

This little lost child's pre-notioned meal was
All prepared, seasoned for him; surfacing
The kitchen with a familiar smell so yummy,
Precisely seared pink inside for his tummy.

But when my grandson sighted his long-
Lost, mourned, and forgotten buried steak,
Drastically quick he bent over, head down,
Wrapping his arms tightly, grabbing abreast.

Startled, perplexed, with an urgent behest,
I urged this doubled-over child to tell fast
Whether he needed an ER trip or just to rest.
His answer poignant: that a knife had dug

Under his ribs and pushed up into his chest.
Easing him gently into my den's recliner, I
Noticed he immediately felt no pain inside.
Investigating his belly, pressuring it slightly,

Such a look of relief enveloped us both.
A distraction was needed. I took the remote,
Handing it to him, ready set for his shows.
This incident reflected exhuming with a hoe

Some ancient, valuable, mourned, forgotten
Day in his past; he felt resolved in knowing
It was long gone; stolen, buried, and rotten.

The shock of it being in a pan on my stove

Caused him physical pain, a PTSD blast.
An accumulation of long tear-dropping days
Was resumed, remembering happy pasts,
As if a shovel dug up and opened a grave.

The intensity lightened with strawberry
Ice cream he assumed Grandma had saved.
Getting his treat, he asked to hold the box
Next to him, eating the flat, smooth top.

Time mellowed, covering over his sadness
Of losing his family, home, school, friends,
Everything he expected belonging to him
That tragically flailed, flung away to an end.

Reminiscing, we two secretly remembered
The moments this grandson never delayed
To run freely across hardwood floors laid
For races, tag chases, jubilant play days.

Also meeting his Grandma at the top of hill,
Jumping into her car for a sleepover thrill,
Occasional pillow fights energizing his will
To perform, jumping as high off the bed tilt.

With a worn-out old mattress still buoyant,
Reaching his arms up to touch the ceiling,
Twirling around and creatively spun, reeling,
Over a course of time he grew tall and lean,

Able to touch the very top of the ceiling.
Years went by, and he never got tired.
He glowed with exuberance for fun desired,
To fill his visit with Grandma, who admired

His lust for life, his laughter, his fire.
He never missed a beat, and he never fell,
Until after the torturing stony night when
His parents were split, he collapsed into hell.

GOD'S HAND was beneath him, and HIS
Plan to redeem this child always in place,
Gradually lifted my grandson, taking him
To a restored life of LOVE, letting smiles in.

GOD'S TIMING IS PERFECTION.
HE IS AN ON-TIME GOD.
WE CAN COUNT ON THE INSTANCE
HE MIRACULOUSLY SAVES,
TAKING AWAY THE DOOM OF THE GRAVE
TO SEND LEGIONS OF ANGELS SWOOPING
US OUT OF TRIALING, STABBING DAYS.

WHICH IS WHY WE MUST ALWAYS
"REMEMBER TO PRAY."
THANKFUL TO GOD FOR NOT SPARING
HIS VERY OWN BEGOTTEN SON,
ELIMINATING OUR DEATH
BY DYING HIMSELF.

SINLESS, EXPLODING LAUGHTER
BESTOWED ON US BY THE LORD GOD,
GRANTING US ENDEARMENT TO SAVOR,
HEALING ALL EARTHLY WOUNDS,
WITHIN US, WITHOUT END,
RESCUED BY BLOOD FLOWING
DOWN A RUGGED TREE, SO ALL BECAUSE OF HIM OUR
HIGHER POWER,
THE ONE WHO CLAIMS:
"I AM."

SO WITH HIS PROMISE, MY GRANDSON,
THERE'S A MANSION SO GRAND,
WITH GOLDEN FLOORS
PAVED JUST FOR YOU TO RUN,
RAMBUNCTIOUS
AGAIN. "REMEMBER TO PRAY"
BELIEVING IN
HIM
✝
✝
✝

Kathryn SchwauSch Branson
6-2-2025

COMPANY

"A letter written for Austin, my Son "
Even God wasn't ambitious
For just Himself
Although everything all was His
He chose not to do it inside an empty nest
God had an intention of being abreast
Man in his image to think on their own
Even if He must sacrifice His dearest SON
He did just to have us with Him
So He created man
To visit in conversation
On His evening stroll
He chose not to be alone
The world's His entity
Why wouldn't HE
He's GOD
He can create anything
EVEN:

"COMPANY"

Kathryn SchwauSch Branson
7-25-2025

CHILDHOOD STOPPED

People are wonderfully MAGNETIZED,
They attach to each other, GLORIFIED,
Latching bodies close together for
ASSURANCE.

Making promises, creating future plans,
Staying close TOGETHER, CONNECTED, ANTICIPATION;
while holding HANDS
And thrilled by each other, taking
UNHEARD-OF "HAPPEN CHANCES."

Relationships are much like dances
Partners stepping close, flowing feet.
They keep the same PACE, and they
NEVER miss a BEAT.

Music and rhythm all harmonious and safe;
They are captured and fascinated
The very moment
They MEET.

Along comes a day without any warning,
One of the partners disarrayed, tangling,
Alarmingly pushing the pining magnets,
Wedging apart AWAY.

The close magnets now start to escape
And scrape at each other, heaving hate.
Did the music start playing off BEAT,
Go dull, become stale
DEFEAT?

Or could it be the family grew and,
Expanding, adding more magnets,
Clashing and hardships mounted,
STILL TIMES THE MUSIC SOUNDED,

Astonishingly beating ABREAST,
With a family passing all of the
Cadence plus
TEMPO
TESTS.

The dance that bloomed in the beginning
Wrestles; clumsy, ungainly, and difficult
To handle; an embarrassing snag in
This once whimsical, now
Wobbly romance.

Maybe a new band could offer advice,
Tell the partners what's gone wrong
In their union as husband and wife,
Helping them reset their magnets,
Bringing in balance, removing
Any such unwanted strife,
A BALLAD brought back
TO LIFE.

IT'S A VERY SAD ONE, THIS TALE,
AS THE BAND WAS MISMATCHED,
WRETCHEDLY LOST BEAT AND FAILED.
Separation began with cracks that split,
FATHOMING CANYONS.

Efforts by all were made to rein back the
Widening gap; but momentum picked up.
CONSEQUENTIALLY, THE MOST DAMAGE
OCCURRED AS THE CHILDREN LAPSED DOWN

THE STEEP, TRICKERY,
SLICK, BIZARRE, WAYWARD
WALL LOST IN THE TRAP.

They live now in the UNKNOWN,
Child magnets needing parental
Match, feeling rejected, wondering,
Lost at the bottom of the ravine gulf,
Without knowing which way they should
Lean or turn or scream or run or just DROP.

SUDDENLY BEING A CHILD COMES TO A

BEDAZZLED

STOP.

Kathryn SchwauSch Branson
5-23-2025

CHRIST-LESS CORNERS

Until I became handicapped and crippled,
I was like an energized maniac physically.
But after losing my ABILITY, my STRIDE,
The MANIAC stayed with me INSIDE.

How does a girl contain trapped energy,
Tied down not lose her mind, stay sane?
This is such a slow process to change;
It's learning to walk from crawling again.

After nineteen back surgeries, all of which failed,
The attempt to restore my step without
Holding tight to another person or rail.

Everything I loved best about life was gone.
I could no longer walk up and down steps
Or trek through the woods with my dog,
So many miles and times of hiking the
GRAND CANYON; those places I didn't
Belong, plus it made people nervous along
With me going sightseeing or even the zoo.

This enclosed world to me is weirdly small,
Must be like a famous movie star or singer
Having a day to go wander about the mall,
To get out in the public, walking, shopping,
Move about effortlessly, NOT STOPPING,
SIGNING AUTOGRAPHS,
Which is somewhat how I feel about me!!

Only difference is, I'm not famous, just hurt.
People gawk at me wherever I go or lurk.
Sometimes they offer to help me, adding

Mostly they say how sorry they feel for me
Having to use my walker. Then I tell them
How utterly thankful and happy I am
To go places, move about, out of bed, be FREE—
Still not invisible though when out,
As people continue to LOOK at me and,
FRANKLY, THEY STARE / THEY GAWK.

I tell them my chances for ever leaving
Bed were quite nil; so now, using a
Walker, I'm so extremely thrilled.
To lighten their look, I tell them that my
Walker is my boyfriend, and I have even
Given him a name, which is: NAUGHTY,
For getting me into trouble now or then.

I tell them how much I love NAUGHTY,
Because it was by GOD'S GOOD GRACE
I could be mobile, vertical, not just talky.
Yet up front, honestly, I pang hunger to walk,
And sometimes NAUGHTY fails me—intense.
Then I stay home on the phone to talk, meaning
The real reason for being shut-in is to balk.

It was at such a time of self-pity when I listened
To Sunday morning WORSHIP—
My son's church service—and that's when
I heard the song: "CHRIST IS ALL I NEED."

Sometimes here, isolated in my house,
Alone, I steal a peek, look around, and
Wonder which "CORNER"
CHRIST IS HIDING IN.
It helps if I look upward toward
The bright light on my ceiling; however,
The glare blocks any vision of angels

Passing by, so I squint my eyes, finding
Out fearfully my vision is blurred and
Remains dimmed, UNTIL once again

Hearing the words of a hymn,
"CHRIST IS ALL I NEED,"
Has inspired me to
Move on and go out to the Eagles Club,
Live music where I am welcomed and
Encouraged to glide out on the floor, try,
WING IT, and tell my walker to PRANCE.

Remembering our motto song for the
Girls who have my same lung disease,
Called lymphangioleiomyomatosis (LAM),
It sings, "To never take BREATH for granted,"
Daring us to give FAITH a fighting chance.
And when we have the choice to sit it out
or DANCE;
We grasp each other's arms
Forming a circular trance
Fearlessly floating across
The ballroom floor
AND DANCE.

Kathryn SchwauSch Branson
<date>

DAISY DELIGHTING MY LIFE

Looking straight ahead, I was facing a
Tall brick wall.
The lane was so narrow it left me no
Room to turn around at all.

Behind me, a large truck was blocking
Me from backing out.
I looked for a driver, but the door was
Locked, and no person in view.

How did this come about?

I thought I was sincere and uplifting,
But then I found out my work was
Crushed down.
Today has been rough, and I'm left
With a frown.

Then, magically, I received a call from
DAISY BROWN.
She is my chief and head promotional
Director in making sure my book is
Published, described as valuable.
And she is spectacular in making sure
That it is displayed all around.

I feel so blessed to have found Atticus;
Their whole team is a well-organized,
Hardworking group of fantastic and
Proficient publishers.

All I can say about them is simply
MAGNIFICENT.
No longer a frown, as they have
Brought me around
To remembering GOOD PEOPLE.

Whenever:

GOD IS IN TOWN.

Kathryn SchwauSch Branson
4-5-2025

DR. WILLIAM HILLNER: HEALING WOUNDED CHILDREN

He listens as with a stethoscope
To their wounded souls.
He notices the cadence,
The strength, the
Entire whole

Of their being to see
If it matches their exterior,
And figures out the query
That is shielded behind
AN ARDUOUS SMILE.

Leaning forward a slight bit,
The doctor softly questions:
"Son, how are you feeling, and
How do you fit in your new school?"

Wondering if this is a trick question,
The boy monotonously replies:
"Everything is fine,"
Even though
Inside he knows that's a lie; but
He hopes it's one THIS DOCTOR
WILL BUY.

Dr. Hillner engages five SENSES
PLUS 6TH,
And his mind volunteers without
Coercion into a field of uncut grass,
Within a border lacking a wall or frame.
He knows astutely well how he has to relay—

Establishing this man's
Ability to casually glide and
Travel over foot-high grass,
Floating and landing smoothly,
Effortlessly CENTERED flat.

Since the answer does not
Match the package that
It is presented in,
DR. HILLNER SURMISES
THESE aren't THE WORDS.
So he softly asks the question,
Yet he puts on a different SPIN.

This time the child is caught off guard,
So he answers
With a TILT
Of his small head, and a look of
CONSTERNATION,
As to what has just been SAID?

Trying to figure out the correct answer
This doctor is looking for,
The child focuses on his softened look,
Yet MATURE, INSIGHTFUL, WONDERING.
But the boy notices that the doctor is very
QUIET. HE IS LISTENING.
He is all ears and ready for the dubious
REPLY.

Dr. Hillner also ascertains the child may be
Squirming a bit
Around about within their seat,
As time itself seems to have been caught
Inside a vault that's locked and has a very
Heavy frame that's blocked.

A moment of silence never hurt anyone,
Then why does it seem to hurt now?
Dr. Hillner calmly sits and sifts this out.
Then he eases in gently, asking another
Question, stating that he is curious about
What the "FINE"
MEANT TO THE CHILD.

Now the child is beginning to PONDER
Within himself the TRUTH,
And studies his own mind as to why he
Is here today, sitting inside this BOOTH.
Dr. Hillner continues to listen INTENTLY,
NON-INVASIVELY but GENUINELY,
SINCERE AND ALERT!!!
He says, "Go ahead, Son; I really want to
HEAR, not to HURT."

This doctor is the expert, so he instinctively
Knows he needs to lead the WAY.
The child quickly runs through his mental
Options as to whether the doctor is simply
CURIOUS or even HOPEFULLY
CONCERNED.

However, the boy notes, could the Dr.'s
Intent somehow allude to trickery,
To catch the boy, thus putting him at bay?
This very "slipped-in" thought itself tells
The child his answer might mean later
HELL-TO-PAY.

CHILDREN WHO ARE WOUNDED EXPECT
THESE TYPES OF DAGGERS,
Hidden within some metaphor that could
Certainly either mean: LESS or MORE

PAIN or COMFORT.
But the child is never literally SURE.

Dr. Hillner could talk all day,
His knowledge and experience
Entirely utmost, vast, and respected.
Heretofore he still knows the answer lives
WITHIN THIS LITTLE BOY,
Who keeps looking and deciphering the
Doctor's face for hints about what path
He must choose now or take in deciding
Those PRECISE WORDS he had better SAY.

Time still trapped inside the vault,
The child already realizes he is sitting
In a foreign place for some good reason.
This isn't like a spelling bee you've spelled
Before, previously learning the answer; nor
Is it racing to secure the see-saw at recess
For time to spend freely with your best pal.

This meeting isn't something breezy.
Seriousness meanders into the room;
Nevertheless, Dr. Hillner chases it away
With his invisible, captivating, enchanted
BROOM thus clearing up the air by
ASKING the boy about his day:
How was it?
When and
Where?

These are concrete, easy questions,
And the child's conversing has begun.
Dr. Hillner listens with full eye contact,
All the while reflecting and speculating
Specific INTONATIONS sung.

The tone of voice has much to say from
Under this little one's hunched-over back.
It often surpasses the words,
Because deep inside of it does dwell a
"FEELING SACK."

A moment of JOY or a stab of DESPAIR—
A CONNECTION IS BEING MADE BETWEEN
"THE DOCTOR AND THE CHILD."
This is the BEGINNING OF "HEALING."
The little wounded boy somehow slips out
A NATURAL CURVED-UP SMILE.

The heavy vault cramping in "TIME"
Cracks open, and then it seems to flow—
Expressing how this talk in time went well.
Our hurting boy does not feel as much
Pain as he felt before, when he first
Walked into Dr. Hillner's DOOR.

THE BOY THINKS TO HIMSELF,
"I may get to visit Dr. Hillner some more."
The child's step is much lighter as he walks
Across the floor, throwing back a glance of
Thanks while expressing acceptance to:

THE MAN WHO LISTENED AND BEAMED,

FASCINATION KNOWING HIM

AS WHO HE WAS FOR.

Kathryn SchwauSch Branson
5-12-2025

EARTH'S FORTUNE

How easy it is to complain
Be dissatisfied unless we see gain

Yet all that we have or possess
Has nothing to do with success

Our total wealth and accumulation
On the dirt that we cross
As we go

Will never be taken with us when we
Are placed in our caskets
Where flowers
Soon grow

Above Our decaying
Broken bodies

The THINGS we hold Dearly we must Know
ARE ONLY THOSE MOMENTS WITH GOD

And the SPIRITUAL times with
RELATIVES and
FRIENDS
OUR 'COMMUNION'
OF "SAINTS"

THOSE WILL TRAVEL ALONG WITH US

IN   THE   END

THAT'S REALLY THE BEGINNING

AGAIN ✠

Kathryn SchwauSch Branson
5-2-2025

EVERLASTING

When you wake, are you glad?

Or when you wake, are you sad?

When I wake, I'm in nagging pain
That hits my perception; I'm MAD.

It dawns on me momentarily,
This pain means LIFE,
Which steers me to ponder on my
LORD and SAVIOR: JESUS CHRIST.

The pain HE endured, OBEYING HIS OWN
FATHER'S WILL,
Was more BRUTAL, HATEFUL, INHUMAN,
SHAMEFULLY, HE WAS DESERTED.

Then, toward the END,
Clinging in a vacuum of LONELINESS,
Taking HIS LAST BREATH
Under HIS OWN FATHER'S WILL.

HE WAS FORSAKEN BY OUR SINLESS GOD,
WHO TURNED HIS PRESENCE AWAY FROM
The searing, scorched, shambled world's
Amassing heap of sin, CRUCIFYING
JESUS, whose name was above ALL.

GOD'S OWN SELF, IN HIS SON, WHO HAD
SWEATED BLOOD WHILE PRAYING,
BEGGING REMOVAL OF THIS BITTER CUP,
But then totally surrendering to HIS
FATHER'S WILL.
Ascending
HOME

Kathryn SchwauSch Branson
<DATE>

FRICK-FRACKING

FRICK-FRACKING AND RETRACTING

SCHWISCH SCHWASCHING

ALL LINES

CROSSING VERTEXING

POLYHEDRONNING

ANGULAR APEXING

3-DIMENSIONAL POLYGONAL FACES

EDGED CLOSE AGAINST SHARP CURVES

PEAKING TIPPING VERTICES

SIMULTANEOUS EXACT

SUCCINCT CONNECTION

THE ALMIGHTY UNIVERSAL LOVE

"SET MATT FREE"

A LUSTROUS SILVER PLATE

LANDED IN YOUR LAP

YOU CAUGHT A GLIMPSE

OF YOUR REBIRTH

THE PLATE SANG OUT A

POIGNANT VERSE

SAYING, "MATTHEW, YOU ARE YOU."

THERE'S NO WAY NOW OF GOING BACK

TRANSPORTED DISTANCES

SKETCHING DOTS

BEFRIENDING OTHERS IN LOVING

YOURSELF

YOU REACHED AND MET

THE LINE BETWEEN PHYSICAL AND

SPIRITUAL TRUTH

PARALLELING COLLIMATE

JUXTAPOSED

THE COLLOCATED VOYAGE

REJOINING

YOU

Kathryn SchwauSch Branson
5-29-2025

FRIDAY DAYS

There is a pillow on my bed turned upward
Nestled next to it, curled in a ball, is FRIDAY,
My grandsons' cat to keep with me for them.
My younger grandson yearned for a cat to stay at Grandma's
for him and his brother
To play with, pet, and carry on visiting day.

Since this would mean a magnificent event,
Considering FRIDAY as the door opened up,
Preparation required resting a lot ahead as
Both grandsons, running in, prohibited cat
Escaping from hugs, swinging, swapping,
FRIDAY, who anticipated boys' love whim.

On days when the boys are not here to visit,
FRIDAY catches up on napping, snoozing,
Relaxing, and lounging in Grandma's house,
Knowing the moment the front door opens,
She will be ecstatic the second she's seen
By grandsons intent for CAT TIME THRILLS.

These are glorious days, boys visiting me.
They were tailor-made days, sleepover stays,
Revolving around FRIDAY, their Tabby cat,
Being luckily retrieved by me from a shelter.
My grandsons had dogs that chased after
Small animals like cats, squirrels, or rabbits.

TREMENDOUS FUN TO LOOK FORWARD TO
WHEN BOYS COULD COME TO VISIT
INSIDE GRANDMA'S BIG HOUSE
ALWAYS SEARCHING TO FIND

"FRIDAY"

CAPTURING HER FOR
FURRY FUN TIME
FLOATING LOVE
MONUMENTAL
MOMENTS IN SPACE
HAPPENING TO TAKE PLACE

ONLY — "ON" — THOSE — BOYS'

"FRIDAY DAYS"

Kathryn SchwauSch Branson
6-9-2025

GOD PLEASE HOLD MY HAND

Disappointed but not defeated

Hurt but not unhealed

Sad but not sorrowful

Confused but not contrary

Hapless but not hopeless

Wondering but not worrisome

Questioning but not questless

Worthless but not unwishful

Sojourning but not unseeking

Left but not left-out

Knowing a heart does not regret

Needy but not unknowing

Dark but not deplorable

Struggling but not surrendering

"Sinful but not unsaved."

Never rending

In the end

GOD HOLDS TIGHTLY TO MY HAND

Kathryn SchwauSch Branson
9-20-2025

GOOD GRIEF: YOU'RE BAD

Why can't grief just be a

ONE NIGHT STAND

Wouldn't it be fine

FORGETTING SORROW

In the very early

WET DEW LIGHT

Why can't grief just

LAST ONE NIGHT

Must it be here when it is not even

SET TIMED RIGHT

Grief amass your wrath,
this instance at once I demand.

Don't show your morbid face, turn it away.

Quit barging in looking to stay.

Sick of you taking all my hopes and all my

TIME, SNATCHING IT

FOR YOUR OWN MAD SAKE

GIVE ME AN EXTENDED BREAK!!!

This is what I have to say to you snarly grief:

AFTER DARK, STOP SNEAKING IN
Setting off my squacking alarm, arousing

ALL MY FRIENDS

Piercing through into my home; my house.

YOU ARE NOT WELCOME

STALKING grief,

YOU'RE A ROBBER; A RANCID THIEF

Dragging hours; gone, your fault, I've lost

MISSING DAYS ALIVE

NOT LIVING ON

Grief wants to trip you up, make you believe
there is nothing now, and everything

NEW WILL SOONER OR LATER

"LEAVE"

Just as it has in your former past,

EVAPORATED

BITTERLY FELT; INVISIBLY SEEN

Grief that overlaps distorts your focus,

YOUR CONSCIOUSNESS

Tearing you in fretful dreams

Any future date with me to smother, smash,

AFFLICTING, CHOKING ME

Forget it grief; my plans with you

ARE A ONE NIGHT STAND

You've been here before.
I'm opening my bolted door.
Don't give me that look

OR YOUR BUTT-IN

I vow to

BOOT
OUT
FOREVER BIDDEN

LISTEN UP:

GET LOST—GET OUT

GOOD /// BAD RIDDANCE

Kathryn SchwauSch Branson
5-28-2025

GREEN

I try my best to live in solitude
Inside a peaceful lonely sanctuary
Where I pretend I'm free
Yet somehow the world keeps
Barging in on me
Will not ignore
Or pardon
My hidden holy empty BE

It interrupts the blinders that
I sneak on to wear
And rudely opens up
Peripheral vision everywhere
At first I twist my neck and
And turn my head away
Yet then I find it on the
Other side I swayed

There is no escaping the world
Or causing it's delay
Casual existence cannot avoid
The Life/Death march we're on

We die to ourselves
Somewhere along this trail
That's when our life begins again
Lifted up we walk away

Our Creator's promise
Does come true
ETERNITY
WINS
Entering Us IN Clean
Exit Signs Blinking
GREEN

Kathryn SchwauSch Branson
9-13-2025

HIDDEN HOPE TREASURE

May be the most intimate
Tie in life for a while.

Coming close; moving apart,
Returning, searching,
Digging the soil

To resolve TREASURES
Buried beneath dirt,
Finding the connections

Between them, wrapped
Around rocks and debris,
Camouflaged at first, then

Found intact, holding

HEARTS INTERBOUND,

Hidden HOPE TREASURES IN

THE GROUND.

Kathryn SchwauSch Branson
5-19-2025

HIGHLIGHTS

Highlights of those
Dreams
Come
True
But wishing on a star won't do.
HIS HIGHLIGHTS cannot be
Torn
Touched
Trampled
On this Earth,
With Angels flying,
Guiding wings,
Misting strong.
Your little one
Does not belong,
In all truth,
NO ONE DOES.
This is just his journey along,
Seeking, searching, singing,
Eyes turned toward
That HEAVENLY place of
Wholeness,
Wellness,
Wonderment,
Worthy of and
Wrapped around,
Within abound,

GOD'S
PERFECT, ENDLESS, FLAWLESS
LOVE.

Written for Asher Timothy Branson by
Kathryn SchwauSch Branson
9-22-2025

HIPPOCRATIC OATH

Some DO and some DON'T
Receive their M.D.'s,
Pledging this OATH
AS A LIFETIME TRUTH.

One day a doctor very well known
Became my PHYSICIAN at a time I felt
Abandoned by most, and I was all alone.
Being welcomed as a patient by this
QUITE KNOWLEDGEABLE
PHYSICIAN,
OFFERING ME COMPREHENSIVE CARE,
EVEN THOUGH MY HEALTH ISSUES WERE
A TOTAL NIGHTMARE,
TAKING ME ONBOARD WAS A BRAVE DARE.

This phenomenal physician kept aboard;
He was at ease when he spoke and kind.
So when he included me into his large,
Challenging practice as ONE of his Pts.,
That relayed an immediate sensation of
Gratitude and relief that took me off guard.

My hopes for acquiring such a revered
Doctor quickly sunk into my mind's eye.
Trying to find the right Dr. was a long roam,
Meandering all about medical professionals.
This man was so NOTABLE; I felt at HOME.

Having survived many near-death ordeals
Made me assume I had already hit rock bottom.
The most flagrant dip I found was yet to come,
My best friend and daughter, a genius great doctor,

Estranged me to live with her friend.
This occurred after a brawl and a split from
Her spouse on a BAD night; she also left ME.
I had been on the top of her white mountain;
I got pushed over, falling off the black side.
My free-falling in darkness left me in a void.

It was during this crushing time of despair,
As my Dr. daughter estranged me, but most
Devastating to me was separating me away
From my two grandsons I had become very
Close to, spending every other week with
Them to help and to play, leading to a fond
Love of them that they exceeded loving me.

Since all my medical Drs. were huge fans
Of my daughter as she was a great Dr. and
Was very looked up to in the hospital I went
To after she changed my health care there,
All of a sudden, overnight, I was deserted.
I certainly never expected to keep my
Primary Dr., for a spectrum of reasons and
Years preceding they worked hand in hand.

A most far-reaching BLESSING from GOD,
When my primary doctor told me with his
Heartfelt sincerity, declaring, "I was his
Patient and HE WAS MY DOCTOR ALWAYS."
After being put from the white to the black
Mountain, my distress so intensely bereft,
This loyal commitment from my main Dr.
Set my hope up on top of a gold mountain.

Because this exceptional doctor stayed
With me when I needed him most just
Seeing his face at appointments SHINES
A LIGHT in my eyes; my HEART was feeling

THE VERY PRESENCE OF GOD,
CAPTIVATING A TRUTHFULLY KEPT
HIPPOCRATIC OATH,
LIFTING MY SPIRIT ABOVE ALL I HAD LOST.

MY DEDICATED DOCTOR KEPT HIS WORD,
CONTINUED TREATMENT IN MY ANGUISH.
MY FOCUS PROJECTED, REMEMBERING
'GOD IS GOOD.' HIS PROMISE TO NOT
LEAVE OR FORSAKE ME WAS REFLECTED
THROUGH AN EXAMPLE OF A GOOD MAN.

MY PHYSICIAN STAYED WITH ME WHEN
OTHERS TURNED ABOUT AND FORSOOK
ONCE AGAIN PROVING

"GOD IS GOOD."

AND WE CAN ALL PEER INTO THE FUTURE,
ETERNALLY LOVED AS

"GOD IS GOOD."
HIS GLORIOUS FAVOR FOREVER
OUTLASTS.

Kathryn SchwauSch Branson
6-3-2025

HORIZONTAL TOLD TALES

Nothing is released or disappears by
rewriting your life's long-lasting history.
You don't know mine, as it's my mystery.
Stay put in your own dark, distorted lane;
leave me out of your loud, shrieking blame.

Past times cannot be changed or erased
by inventing emotionally charged stories.
Turbulent dishonesty becomes unfurled,
crushing your goodness and your glories;
brashness reveals your emptiness hurled.

Precious memories suffer loss if glazed;
rare moments carved inside your heart
are much too valuable for you to depart.
Yours exclusively should not be cast away;
invisible ink may hide reality, but still it stays.

Indubitably, those events hang on to remain,
slipping out of your swayed world one day.
No person escapes them or scampers away,
friends are crushed, thrown on a pile of all
the others you tossed before, there to lay.

This will not appear full view in your mind,
as selective memory loss makes you blind.
For what cause you feel forced to heave
out distorted bits of tainted verbal deceit,
yesterday holds facts untouched and real.

A crafted memento or cheap ornament
is nothing more than an archaeological
declared eminence, hewn jagged small,

shards crumbling from a sham artifact,
restructured decadence blown up to fall.

Choking reality for all, a brief suffocation
inevitably does not last or pass inspection.
Facts can be misspelled and feelings sunk
underwater, but truthful events can't be
dunked; being buoyant, they rise atop sea.

This wasted effort of puffed-up arrogance
hardens, passing into a state of concrete,
resurfacing madness and pain so mean,
meant to demolish loved ones wiped clean,
returns home to you distraughtly, a breach.

Robbing you of the love you could have had,
sadly it's missing, and you're void of any joy.
Gaining was losing; giving wasn't receiving,
the gloating interfered, yelling a dull noise;
love to recycle, you blocked stark in ending.

All the deepest identity a person could gain
is bestowed by His handiness in creation.
Now the bubble burst, and foibles remain;
where are all your subjects praising fame?
They can't find, as worth no longer remains.

The answer strictly lies in God, who never
changes day after day; He is our sole claim.
He is the constant of yesterday, today, and
tomorrow, striding onward to eternal hope
for everlasting life, perfect in God's hold.

We shudder, taking chances on losing His
undeserved heaven because our minds
keep trying to reach a mental resolution,

thus, being human, we misunderstood
how loftier He is than our world ever could.

The Tower of Babel fell apart, as it should;
we must look up to Him, in confusion dazed.
His glory is so great we couldn't achieve
making sense or comprehension of such
wondrous love; He only asked we believe.

We speculate it must require so much more;
His infinite resilience was simply a cross.
Only God could endure this monumental
save in shedding His holy Son's blood,
flowing down for us to be with Him above.

THIS IS OUR

DIVINE ✝

GOD'S

LOVE

Kathryn SchwauSch Branson
7-15-2025

HOW ALONE FEELS

This Is How Lonely Feels

A person surrounded by black walls,
no one around to hear
if they stumble or fall,
questioning themselves
if this life of theirs remains actually real,
imagined or dreamt up,
so quiet, so still.

Not another one's thoughts
to reflect off their will,
if will is even yet alive,
part of them, or is it nil.
If no one's around
to notice or see, we become
anxious, afraid to stir up the air;
we drift about, lost in a drained, empty quill.

There is no response or call from our Giver;
our ears tune out sound waves that quiver.

If this is one of God's jokes
He plays so we'll visit
Him intently in private,
our heartaches to spill,
we can give it a shrill
voice, screaming our fears,
blasting out God's ears,
waiting for a rebuff,
His answer that gives us
a divine way to fix
all of our ills.

He's promised to listen
to each word that we speak.
He knows how we harbor needs
inside ourselves, trying to keep
ashamed of ourselves; yet
God is open to all our hidden secrets.
He will faithfully never deny us relief,
as He sees below the surface
of life's water trough,
green from all the shifting algae
hovering over us on the top.

Nothing blocks His view;
His eyes can see clear, clean through.
His optimal precision envisions our
entire existence, as His sight goes beyond
this earth's indiscernible hue.
His eyes shift around along all of our paths,
the twists, the turns, and the warps,
following the torques of our travels,
blocking offensive slants meant to veer
us off course from evil interventions meant
to dispute His purpose in arrows of lament,
drowning us in our sorrows, forsaking our
Savior, who is our constant encouragement.

We beg and deplore if God meant His sheep
to feel bitter loneliness, hiding in retreat.
His answer is in His Word, the Bible He gave,
allowing us to give full attention aimed at
the powerful wisdom written down to save
our empty spirits from needless dismissal
of God's secure, loving arms He installs,
holding out to us every day, for us to chase
away any gray, unwarranted cold chests,
shivering when we can't feel Jesus' caress.

Praying for our Lord to slide loneliness into
God's pockets and far up His sleeve,
thus enlightening our minds
and our hearts to receive
our Comforter's warmth,
honoring us when
we come to
BELIEVE.

Kathryn SchwauSch Branson
7-25-2025

IRON HORSE

Russell Rode Up to Heaven on a Fast Rail

My brother had an unusual attraction
to all trains, as he was spellbound intently,
fascinated, enthusiastic, and enthralled,
about this earth, sparking understanding:
why it moved, how it worked, and landed.

My brother's mind was a deep well;
he aspired to fill it with the entirety
of everything that caught his attention.
His face lit up at anything he questioned;
the smallest iota of beauty captured
his assiduous notice and contemplation.

Russell, my brother, was a gentle soul.
He owned my inborn heart with his hold.
He needed me to recount his lost childhood;
it seems that the thunder and pouring rain
in our home life, within torn nuances, tugged
at his memory bank in a raging flash flood.

Much of his youth swept his memory by,
the uneasy, chaotic darts and flaring-out blasts.
Because my mind had open spaces, not like
my brother's continuum of mysteries had,
encircling him in a skybound imagination,
I was able to absorb our youth to offer back.

His death left me here, cold, misunderstood;
no one ever loved me so deeply as he could.
I long to sit, holding hands, rolling our tears.
Russell was a brightly lit torch of power;

wherever he went fell glistening showers.
How will I survive in life without him here?

We two were intertwined and connected,
yet our beings were different in all aspects.
My arms are empty, not wrapping his neck.
Please show your face, my brother dear;
give me your smile and come down here.
Visit with me intimately, touching me near.

I promise to release hold and let you go,
but first, my Lord,
hear my prayer.
I NEED YOU BRO 🙏

Kathryn SchwauSch Branson
7-21-2025

IT'S NOT OVER TILL IT'S OVER

THE STANCE
THE STRIDE
THE GLEAM
IN THEIR EYES

GEARING UP
GAME SOON STARTS
EXHILARATION SPARKS

Teammates PRANCING in a TRAIN
Enthusiasm ESCAPES RESTRAINT
Legs SPRINGING UP without REIN

SPECTATORS ARRIVE
BAGPIPES ARE SOUNDING
SCOTS GATHER HUDDLING IN
THE CHANT LEANING BEGINS:

SHA SHA GOR'EE
SHA SHA KAVUSA
SHA SHA KALUNGA
SHA SHA SHA-VANGA
KOOM-MWEYA
KOOM-MWEYA
"GO SCOTS!"

CAPTAINS LINE UP
SHOULDER TO SHOULDER
PADDOCKED ENERGY SMOLDERS

Players enter the field in place;
the KEEPER PRAYS on GOALPOST,
his back turned inward with FACE.

A WHISTLE IS BLOWN,
there's a SCATTERING with SHOUTS;
the field SWIVELS, PIVOTING about.

At first there exists careful
ENDEAVOR to be ACCURATE;
soon TENSION pushes PACE to RACE.

The SOCCER BALL
is the TARGET of SIGHT;
no one is STILL, all are ALIVE.

INSIDE the GOAL,
the KEEPER is STEPPING, WINGING;
he STOPS the BALL, then he LEAPS,
LEFT-FOOTED, KICKING.

The game is a PUZZLE,
a CHESS MOVE with MUZZLES.
Shooting KICKS LAND; the BALL
INSIDE the NET BUSTLES.

Each TEAM is SCORING;
the wild ONLOOKERS APPLAUD, ROARING.
PRECISE FOOT THRUSTS CONTINUE DARTING;
PLAYERS are SWEATING,
BREATHING is POUNDING,
RAPID HEARTBEATS RESOUNDING.

HALF TIME for a BREAK plus a PLAN,
WATER is DRUNK, THROWN, and SPLASHED;
REPOSING is MOMENTARY before a DASH.

The SCOREBOARD may be
SQUEEZING or ELLIPSING;
COMBAT RESUMES on STEAMING.

The VIBRATORY RESONANCE
STIMULATES ABSURD ANTICS;
BODIES COLLIDE and FLIP.

A PLAYER is DOWN,
SILENCE PERVADES; not a SOUND.
INJURY RESOLVES as the CROWD
CLAPS, ECHOING RELIEF ALOUD.

RESILIENCE and STRENGTH MAINTAIN;
ENDEAVOR is ALL in THE GAME.

From BEGINNING to END,

THE STANCE
THE STRIDE
THE GLEAM
IN THEIR EYES

GOD IS IN COMMAND
"IT'S NOT OVER TILL IT'S OVER."

GOD'S WILL STANDS.

Kathryn SchwauSch Branson
10-13-2025

JADE

Some people are jewels;
they make other people's pain dwindle.
So one might ask, how is this done?
First of all, by offering the despondent person
a feeling of hope for the return of a scammer's
gain, who conquered their savings through
treacherous swindle.

Those works of help and
acts of love
completely baffle the suffering,
exploited person with
surprise and elation
as they attempt to comprehend
how some unknown other, with a
desire to return their loss and
help them to regain,
surely exemplifies the way of our
Lord's earthly fame.

He brings to followers kindness
and wonderment,
mirroring the sweetest voice of a girl
with the most befitting, beautiful name,
whom others she knows call the
benevolent, joyful Jade,
which barely reflects her radiant glaze.

These are the people and moments
during our lives
we must ponder upon,
remember, and follow
their lead as we get lost in the haze

of rushed and hapless, hurried days,
skimming this world's
shallow understanding.

God's command for us to carry within,
bringing us through and out
of the fog, leading our bodies to
safety for the goal
of caring for others, while the
echo resounds
as truthful and deep as this time once done
for us with compassion and caring.

In a young girl's daily works, her way of
tossing kindness bravely, commending,
attesting, epitomizing her memorable,
exquisite name: "Jade."
Which, spiritually, is said to symbolize
beauty, wisdom, and serenity,
being associated with good luck.
ILLUSTRATE

Written for Jade by Kathryn SchwauSch Branson
10-15-2025

JOY IS WHAT?

Joy is delight in the undelightful

Joy is pleasure in and around pain

Joy is wanting to cry but laughing then

Joy is being okay with misery

Joy is lead spilled on this page

Joy is fear underneath courage

Joy is inside the eye of the hurricane

Joy is sitting on top of the windmill

Joy is embracing regret as learning

Joy is a clean shiny linoleum floor

Joy is hugging your dirty dog's neck

Joy is swinging back and forth

Joy is giving up sadness

Joy is limping but still walking

Joy is remembering past successes

Joy is expecting more blesses

Joy is spots from your fountain pen

Joy is writing clean lines again

Joy is PERMANENT

Joy is not temporary happiness

Joy is focusing on your LORD

Joy is kicking satan out the back door

Joy is wanting to dance to music

Joy is music 🎶 🎹 🎵

Joy is feeling fine as the dance is over

Joy is knowing you married the right one

Joy is believing your spouse is GOD'S

Joy is forgetting about giving up

Joy is having way too much to do

Joy is having anything to do

Joy is blowing off technology

Joy is glad technology blew you off

Joy is painting your walls with your Soul

Joy is ink stains streaking your arms

Joy is anticipating it will wash out

Joy is a dream that is not a nightmare

Joy is a nightmare ending when you wake

Joy is caring about someone else

Joy is caring about yourself

Joy is declaring all human rights

Joy is not belonging to a group

Joy is being grouped in GOD

Joy is a thing you love to seek

Joy is finding Joy in a blizzard

Joy is God's present to everyone

Joy is when His SON delivered

US

JOY IS THUS

Kathryn Schwausch Branson
9-20-2025

INFINITY

Endlessness single moments
that attach to each other, creating
a strand of glory once received
from a dash of time through the gift of
another, whose feelings were kind,
symbolizing harmony, virtue, eternity,
balancing the scale of higher beings.

As some cultures revere it to be
a stone of the gods, sacred to the heart,
called chakra:
a place and an organ of love
that each life possesses while naked,
to be clothed in robes of silk,
purest, velvety green.

While wearing this nature and temperament,
continue to pass on and
illustrate and fate.

LIMBO FROG

Took Away and Kept Away

After eight long, empty months,
up until the time called finalizing divorce,
thinking the war was over, with no winners,
dearth and paucity devising themselves to come.

My youngest Chattanooga grandson,
often at my house he stayed,
for our private overnight adventures.
All his choices, all his play,
as all declared: his day.

Filet mignon was the pick of his pleasure
for supper, with baked potato in butter.
Frozen orange juice he himself made,
perfecting the amount of water to use,
stirring fervently until it came out smooth.
Of course, a large tray to accommodate Heinz 57,
sauce covering a fourth of the plate.
This was his tradition,
no exceptions to the rules.

A pillowcase tablecloth draped
over the cat stand, which my grandson
physically put together with his own hands.
Being in the den, the TV remote was given to him,
a regular celebration, like an Olympic event!

What on God's fallen, dreary earth
ever happened then?

January 20, 2023, clocks began cracking.
They all started going backward
in a most deceptive, premeditated, revengeful way.

No reason my grandsons ever imagined
that their familiar childhood days,
visiting Grandma and their cat, Friday,
or growing up in their childhood home,
would reach a roadblock, crashing into a
dead end,
held under the ruins of the wreckage.
No way to crawl out,
no hope to save the day,
nor attempting escape.

Severance and damage under the
umbrella emotion: beneath it is anger,
seething, steaming, growing.

God performed miracles and rescued
many flip-flops from disastrous heydays.
Divorce was ended,
but the war would stay.

Grab your shovel and dig up your grave,
dust yourself off as you pitch dirt away.
Believe you can survive, believe in a new
day coming around God's bend,
on the road that never dead-ends.

Raise your hands and call the name: JESUS.
He keeps you forever hidden from view,
but you feel Him inside you His Spirit
lives within you, as you are His home.
There is no more loneliness;
God has all things

covered for you with
His enduring
love and protection,
embracing you.

Using His pierced hands, He designs
your new life's plan,
including smiles and laughter,
security consistent. Your Lord
shapes you and molds
you the way He made you,
once again,
✝
Whole.

Kathryn SchwauSch Branson
5-31-2025

MAMMA'S MICKEY

"Hermann, quick! Get the shotgun!
Go shoot Mickey, he appears to
have contracted rabies!"

My brother Russell, my cousin Darrell, and
I were watching, frozen, in our screen porch,
huddled together tightly, close in a daze.

Mickey was running around in wild circles,
projecting slime and slobber, choking froth
spewing out bubbling foam from his mouth.

Hermann, my daddy, quickly moved about
to grab his twelve-gauge, placed in his closet
at the back end of our old wooden house.

My cousin Darrell was, to us, like a brother,
so much together we became to be known
by our alias as "The Three Amigos."

With Darrell's childhood were times alone;
he was scarred, pained, wounded, and lost.
Our grandparents rescued him as their own.

Otto and Alma also took care of Russell
and me when Mamma left to work in a blitz
at the Georgetown Hospital as an anesthetist.

Often we Three Amigos were at our farm;
again we three spent time too at Grandpa's.
So our childhoods coincided, hand in arms.

Mickey's startling event was at our house,
this was our first old home on our big farm.
Beside the landing was the big screen porch.

We three kids stared at Daddy and Mickey,
stumbling about, kicking up gravel, chasing
each other in our backyard a sight to see.

Mickey was Mamma's tubby Chihuahua,
who was happiest eating all he could get.
The problem was within him, and it was set.

That day evolved, a rare scene, utmost odd.
There was tension and fear in all our hearts;

we Amigos stared agape, dreading the plot.

We pushed close up onto the porch screen.
We'd never seen rabies or a dog blown to bits;
it had to be done, as rabid animals are mean.

Suddenly, frantically
Irene, my Mother, yelled out to our Daddy,
a screeching loud:

"STOP!
Hermann, don't shoot my Mickey,
he has gobbled raw okra I picked in a big pot!"

Eating raw okra causes a foaming mouth.
We Three Amigos let out our held-in breath,
easing a sigh of relief from facing such a
close call of seeing Mickey shot to death.

We imagined foam and a Mickey explosion,
being slain by a twelve-gauge gun, close range.
It was a devastating image to us that day.

Mickey recovered, and my mother never
left buckets of vegetables out uncovered
on the back porch where we would gather.

It was a place we shelled black-eyed peas,
or roller-skated and pulled our red wagon,
and where Irene's ringer washtub cleaned.

For the Three Amigos, the rest of our day
was filled with fun as we explored the farm.
We had not forgotten the imminent harm.

Mickey meandered, searching for more food;
he was fat and ravenous, we all understood.
His cravings were inborn so nothing to do.

A Chihuahua shouldn't weigh twenty-five pounds!
Irene snuck him small treats to let him eat.
He was shaped like a little barrel with feet.

The truth of all creatures, large or small,
is that they have their own personal seat,
their role in life, their own drum to beat.

God asked us to manage all of the animals,
being kind and merciful, even if they were
eventually food on our suppertime tables.

All living things on God's earth
deserve mercy given by man,
whom God placed in charge
over the entire land.

We are never to forget,
all of life came from and truly belongs in

GOD'S

ALMIGHTY

COMPASSIONATE

HANDS

Kathryn SchwauSch Branson
7-23-2025

MIDDLE GROUND

This is a story revolving around

MIDDLE GROUND.

The World's Earth Is Really Flat

It's just that
all the people moving in search of the edge
of the World's Earth have levered so much
weight, it caused the World's Earth to
begin to bow and bough down.

On the other side of the flat World's Earth,
so many people moving in search of the edge
of their flat World's Earth levered so much
weight also, causing it to bow and bough
down.

Thus, the edges of the flat World's Earth
bowed and boughed down until they
reached each other, forming a circle.

This is when the flat World became
the round Earth.

When this union occurred, the Earth
forever remained round.
It remained round as all
the people of this World kept searching
in circles, spinning it around.

The circles made a very big difference
to our World's Earth.

The main difference is that no longer is it
precisely possible to ever find the authentic.

MIDDLE GROUND

Kathryn SchwauSch Branson
7-27-2025

MILESTONE

A mountain so high it is
Out of your eye's range
There are a number of paths
And beginning choices of trails
You wonder which one is the
One you're meant to take

Then you silently seek God
Asking Him for help in this
Difficult decision you must make
The answer may very well be easy
Or turn out a grueling mistake
Others around you are

Already gone away
God shifts your eyes on the
Trail He desires you choose
In the beginning the trail is
Surprisingly easy and smooth
The dirt is dry allowing you to walk straight

But abruptly soon becomes slippery slate
The Spiritual sign of this metamorphic rock
Is utilizing inner body plus energy to stock
God prepares you for your journey
This course will be most extraordinary
Occurring to you while climbing boulders

Sidestepping fallen trees as your shoulders
Ache forming blisters from straps on your
Back with supplies in a pack lifting it over
Surging forceful streams gushing water
Boots get soaked and your clothes cling
To your body with a stabbing cold sting

You're questioning what God's got you in
Soon you're forgetting the Prayer you gave
Entreating God's help this decision to make
Now not praying your hope is for shortcuts
That may ease your way in proceeding up
Your survival or reaching the top suggests

You must Pray once again asking for JESUS
Remembering His own trail also felt weary
Your query to Him was how to avoid dreary
This valley was God's true way for you to go
He said to step on this long valley so slow
Taking hold of God's hand you continue on

You're all by yourself only your Maker along
God holding your hand makes you strong
When your legs feel weak God says PAUSE
He places you on His lap to ease your load
Have food to eat before you rise to the road
Pray with ME for a while in thankfulness

For sustenance and love and time to rest
Your solis with The Holy Spirit gives peace
Plus assurance and The Light that you need
This is your portion in life following HIM
You are to pick up your cross and begin
Up this rugged hill as Jesus took to Calvary

Burden too heavy God's Yoke you will carry
He said His burden was easy His yoke light
Accepting The Cup sweating blood in fright
Like Jesus turning your Will to God in night
Is the most tempting time to give up not try
Go face your adversary agree to God's Will

He's granting Yahweh's mercy going up Hill
God's purpose for you is saving your Soul
Giving you victory His free love bestowed
The trail you picked was Eternity bound
Your back will be raw blood oozing down
Believe in GOD as HE has believed in you

All temptations trials He'll get you through
March on ahead a Christian Soldier you are
Baring your cross up to the top not very far
Failing tired you fall down on this sojourn
Help comes your way as there is no return
Finish this climb trudging upward fatigued
Once you reach the top your life is freed

Your Milestone a great accomplishment
The trail you chose very few others went
Stake your flag on top of this mountain
Your walk with GOD outweighed most
Who lacked courage to join The High Host
Your test has been humbly won

Now GOD'S Fountain go find
Heaven was your's when you
Chose THE LORD
As your Soul
GUIDE

Kathryn SchwauSch Branson
7-27-2025

MOURNING MORNING

Do You Mourn Morning?

Do you mourn morning because you
dread the day ahead,
or do you mourn morning
because you miss the night you left?

Nights are healing, filled with dreams,
and snuggling times for imaginings.
Days can be battlefields with bitterness,
damaging verbal rebuttals that scream.

The question is still: Why
mourn morning?

It is the dawn of a new day; anything can
happen to come, good or bad, your way.
If your mind is set on taking this whole
business of life with a positive stride,

then waking up doesn't really matter,
as you have nothing to fear or hide
from entering your day's awake time,
knowing full well it's up to you to decide.

You can determine your own investigation,
if this day is dull or filled with invigoration.
Thus, at the end of the day you will find
it has mostly boiled down to this bottom line:

Somewhere in your head are switches
you can flip up or flip down as you choose.
The strangest thing about these switches
is they possess power for a win or a lose.

So the question is answered: Why
mourn morning?

Since life comes upon you anyway,
without any wake-up warnings,
why not give it your best shot.

and welcome in
a blinding, bright,
shining all is right
Good morning to morning!

Without giving notice to any
mourning, fear, or fright.

AS GOD GOT YOU THROUGH
ALL LIGHTLESS LAST
NIGHT

Kathryn SchwauSch Branson
6-2-2025

OFF THE HOOK

God, I'm Very Tired and Feel Small

God, I'm very tired and feel small.
My family life is rubbing me raw.
Will You let me off the hook?

Is there anyone on earth I can call,
who desires to listen?
My pain is cutting me so deep;
it runs through my chest like a skill saw.
I see no blood, no skin, no broken bones;
this pain is hidden, buried inside my soul.
God, will You please let me off the hook?!

If You tell me no, I will turn my face and look
up toward Heaven to seek Your angels' help.
I myself am way too intertwined within my own
drained, limp, mummified, out-to-pasture self.
I lack the courage that You ask firmly of me,
so I'm begging of You to set me free to be.

Yet I know inside my riddled body
Your omniscience speaks: I must obey.
I believe in You, my Lord, my Savior-King,
so hand me the cup and guide me to pray,
"Thy will be done," this very day.

No person here thinks I am strong enough.
But God, I'm not counting on myself
to get this job done.
I'm counting on You to lift me up.
I'm counting on You to build me up.
I'm counting on You to help my grandsons.

I'm counting on You to stop rotten fear
from claiming it's won.

The victory belongs to You, my Lord,
my Savior, my King Jesus Christ.
You suffered much more than any human
on earth could touch, muse, meditate, or bear.
You were not forced, You drank to save
my woeful, sinful, disobedient, wavering life
through Your gracious, beautiful flesh,
suffering and incomprehensible strife.

How can I be so scant a person
who bemoans my situation and cries for myself?
Dear Lord, my God, dry away my pity tears.
Help me to trust You, always ever near.
Take my arm, my hand, my will, my self;
thrust me this cup, and I'll hold it strong,
willing, courageous, without any spills.

It's no more than a faucet turned on low,
but without Your divine help, even that
small amount of flow I cannot control.

I'm writing You this letter, my
Almighty God.
You've given me the answer.
You've decided not to let me off the hook.
I've decided to lean on Your love and
hook into You.

As You lead me into battle's harm, help me
to fight the evil one who has decided to
drive me down
and block my belief, forcing me to turn, run.

To him I say:
"Get behind me, Satan.
Get thee hence.
Go away."

Tuck Yourself and Your Demons' Tails

Tuck yourself and your demons' tails
under your rumps.
I will climb this barbed-wire fence,
no piercing of my flesh I'll feel, because
You, Lord, will guide my hands and feet.

Barefoot and brave, I know what to do:
I must pray and seek Your wisdom
to live yet again another day,
to continue obeying Your
Salvation's holy way,

of loving and caring and risking myself,
as You direct me and lead my steps to
do Your will with no concern for whom
it upsets! On earth we have one way to
move: to follow our Maker and make do
with the bodies we have, though they aren't new.

We house the Holy Spirit to take us
through all lonesome valleys and
over rugged, unknown terrain.

God is love and redemption and life.
Remarkably, nothing can hold me back.
That's because God gives no slack
in His power giving strength I lack.

Forgive me, God, for whining to be
"let off the hook."
I was shallow and weak, not believing
"You never forsook"

a person who sought Your WILL and
humbled themselves to obey.

This challenging path ahead,
God, push me Your way.
Jump-start my engine;
I struggle with my key
that's stuck in me.

Ignite my desire to do Your will.
I need You, Lord; I haven't the skill.
With angst and depression I am still
just an empty, cracked-up shell.

For turning around a child's suffering,
their lives torn, shrill,
I beg of You, God, that I never flinch.
There's work to be done,
help me roll up my sleeves.

Lord, get me out of this chair!
Launch me into Your world.
Help me to do as You need.

Prepare me,
I plead.

Kathryn SchwauSch Branson
6-6-2025

⏰ GOD'S ON—TIME JUMPER CABLES

Life on Wheels Stopped

No, it just stalled.

Being early, I pulled over to wait,
turned on my emergency lights.
Now it's time to go but my battery's dead.

Mom is already at the airport!!

I'll run into the middle of oncoming traffic,
wave my hands wildly over my head.

Hey! This is veritably working,
some gutsy driver just made
a daring, reckless U-turn.
What was he thinking??

He heads in my direction.
I dash back to my car.
He stops and looks for detection,
a laboring lady maybe having a baby
in the back seat or on the floorboard.

What other answer would be valid
for why this guy was in the middle of traffic,
wildly swinging arms at whizzing-by cars?

He swung around in my direction, asking,
"Can I help you, sir?"
"I am a man driving for Uber."

Thank God, thinks my son, as he asks,
"Do you happen to have jumper cables
in the trunk of your car?"

The man responds,
"Sure thing, buddy. What's the
emergency they're for?"

Austin blurts out, out of breath,
"My mom's at the airport,
she can't walk, she's disabled."
"Plus she is old, and she's feeble."

Perhaps the Uber man is thinking
she most likely is unreasonable and needy.

Austin gasps, "I'm supposed to be there to
help her get out of the airport wheelchair,
find her walker and lift her up shotgun,
riding back to Lake Geneva,
the town I am from!"

When I heard my son's story,
it impressed me that he
would risk his life to be
on time for me—whose
motto in life was always:

Showing up late or just flying
on in, driving right past the gate.

Since we were both still alive,
different reasons for that,
Austin drove up precisely on time.

My luggage was circling around a long line.
He spotted my walker down on its side,
exhausted, no doubt, from airplane travel,
with bags being tossed this way and that.

My suitcase soon followed; we were, at last,
all set in my son's still-running car
for the anticipated excursion.

Hannah had well planned and arranged a
visit focused on Grandma with grandkids,
lots of hugs and bright eyes blinking, lit up.

We embarked for this special event.
A Family Coming Together

GOD Smiling - His timing turned out

Just as ☀ HE MEANT

Kathryn SchwauSch Branson
7-26-2025

OPTIONAL LIFE

When I woke up this morning exhausted
That nagging question mark
Of whether to stay in or check out
Did not surface to my mind as a choice

Life dawned on me not as an optional route
Mine doesn't verily allow discretion to last
Being created by GOD , He has the final
Say-so in writing about all future or past

People joke about how GOD threw the
Mold away after making them unique
I can say it without any contradiction
No one can easily describe my oblique

State of flawed personality or weak traits
That carry me through time and space
God handed me life on a warped plate
Those I'm in contact either love me or hate

Coming off the assembly line my passage
And experiences to many appear weird
Never occurring to them they're standing
Right next to me strangely looking queer

I would suppose to interject the issue
Might be more related to the people near
Me and connected to their energy source
So really whose shoe wobbles and veers ?

I don't try to be eccentrically passionate
It comes entirely unintentional and natural
The only time I am fast is when I am late
Not much about my life is normal or dull

Once my eyes open up I grope out the gate
My main concern is survival as it's my fate
To be in positions involving push and pull
If I feel weak alone I know Jesus is my mate

Kathryn SchwauSch Branson
7-17-2025

PINNACLE

So much joy is lost in search of our 'before'

On days we felt strong with allies close by

Staying near us with acceptance smiles

All the while, expecting 'more'

Can we maintain focus from

Some famous person's eye

No one tarries high in their

History's lustrous limelight

Our daily sun arises all our years

With equally precise brightness

Time has quickly marched on by

Like soldiers stepping briskly

Toward a stopping point

Where they arrive

To rest or die

Dimness shades across our sight caused

By hours and days of aging - not by night

Can we mellow in the years we've reached

Even though we tend to stagger moving so

Slow wearing flat shoes on our aching feet

Can a well worn arm chair dipping low from

Gracing us; serving many years as our seat

For decades ,calendars, and daily planners

Shredded piles of memory slits; truly be

Replaced by a brand new unweathered

Modern lounger for us to proudly sit ?

All living things will someday

Over time reach their top peak

From that day on they fade and

Ease down a sticky slope so steep

Until we've all mastered crossing over

Our own mountain where we

Finally come to greet a

Plot on level ground

Being dug for our

Burial beneath

We must remember while we live before

The day our Maker comes for us to meet

How markedly true our source of joy

Was never granted by this earth , but

Instead by our Lord's Salvation we can

Celebrate with blood in wine and bread

Taken in Sacredly; savored Holy Sweet

Consider the way we conquered trails

Hopefully while helping others to rise

Above dangers, hardships, or defeat

Did we lock arms within their walk

Aiding them by joining in their valley

Trudging out of mud holes dipping deep

None of us are strangers here if our aim

Seeks pointing up to GOD'S GLORY SEAT

Where our Spirits live with Angels praising

THE ONE; while we humbly bow and kneel

In wondrous anticipation for Jesus's return

When our still bodies will be

Restored shining sinless

Sharing life with DIVINE

Beyond earth's ticking

Menace here ; existing

In a fallen world to be

Miraculously healed

Freely forgiven by

Our SAVIOUR'S shed

BLOOD; SON OF GOD

AND SON OF MAN

To take us HOME

Immortally

Pure

We are

SEALED ✞

Kathryn SchwauSch Branson
7-8-2025

PINK LEMONADE

Brenda, Completely Still

Brenda, completely still,
awake, staring up with an empty, blank look.
Sitting next to her, my insides churned.

She was my first patient as a student nurse,
a summer job at the Shriners Burns
Hospital for Crippled Children.

I had no idea what I was to do.
The head nurse said, "Sit next to her.
She is new."

Her body was covered in white bandages,
up to the very edge of her chin and jaw.
She had the most smooth, lovely skin
covering a child's pristine, delicate,
oval, doll's-porcelain face.

I was frozen afraid to move, tensely still.
She was burned all over,
keeping only a trace
of untouched, intact, unscorched,
healthy, useful skin.

Both of us barely breathing,
scarcely alive.
Brenda was near death from fire;
I was near death, caught in the air
between us.

Neither one of us knew if we'd make it out
or ever see life again.

Hours of time trapped us thus in this state.
I knew and she felt alone and unsafe.
I felt helpless to reverse her fate.

Finally, a nurse came in and told me
I could go then.
I whispered, "Goodbye," and said,
"I'll see you again."

Brenda glanced with her eyes and blinked.
This was the first day of being in touch,
a time together for us,
coming to grips with a foreign,
extraneous, brand-new world
for a tiny being's destroyed, spoiled body.

To begin a lifelong journey of healing,
neither one of us knew about tomorrow.
We both were aware there'd be sorrow.
The stillness of that day and our closeness
comes into my mind without thinking,
a fleeting greeting of souls remeeting.

Sharing a passage we'd travel and discover,
a new way to exist in our lives we would
ever remember, and never recover.
I've kept the feel of the quiet, muffled
unknown until forever, into time to fly.
We shared, all alone, motionless, subdued,
without expressing grief or unhappiness,
yet downcast and smothered, breathing.

It was a time of peace, preparing Brenda
for the pain-filled next span to breach.

Years of her life altered from normal,
growing up in a children's hospital,
re-piecing her outward appearance
with skin grafts and slits for growth,
all brought about from a flammable
nightgown. Dancing and playing with
her brother, when a spark from the
fireplace darted out of the hearth,
striking her lace dress as she was hopping,
igniting a fire, flames all-consuming,
this happy girl's dancing into screaming,
terror of pain in horror, then stopping.

Wrapped in blankets, awaiting an
Ambulance, a glaring sound arriving
quickly as possible on the scene.
Calls were made; the EMTs and paramedics
requested helicopter transport for an
airlift, and Brenda was carefully lifted
and taken to the most hopeful place to
save her small life on this saddest of days.

She was flown to Galveston U.T.M.B.,
Shriners Burns Hospital,
her new home and a specialized team
awaiting, prepared to redeem
the life of a child lost by a beam
of light from a glowing fire,
stealing her body, her future, her dreams.

Life had to start wholly over,
as her skin had melted within moments.
It takes years to patch up and heal.

Every day that I worked, I would see her and
say how special a patient she'd always be.

Her mother moved to live close with
other mothers nearby, so their child
could be seen, comforted, and soothed.

One day I noticed the ladies sitting
around in a circle, all chatting, crooning.
The topic of lemonade came up, and I
accidentally blurted out: "Pink!"

For an eventful, delightful treat,
having pink lemonade with ice to drink.

Brenda heard me, and she became
unusually, exceptionally excited.
She was smiling, unfettered, and started
begging her mother to please go get
some from a nearby store right away.
Her eyes were bright as she gleefully
Pleaded but her mother said,
"Not today. Maybe tomorrow, or some other day."

The ladies were all in the middle of gossip,
conversation huddled together, bonding,
and did not care for interruption of their
new-formed mothers' club of belonging,
with others who had moved from home
to be near the hospital so their child
wouldn't live for so many months all alone.

I watched Brenda's smile fall swift to the
floor and turn downward, facing the ground.
Desperate to leave myself, but I was on duty.
It was beyond my ability to comprehend

denying this burned-up little darling,
such a simple request to feel joyfulness,
seldom or randomly happening to know.

The rare chance of anticipation to eagerly
capture a nuance of celebration for the
chance of getting to sip from a magical glass,
filled with a treat of iced effervescence, on
a mystical, most enchanting, finest of days.

CHEERING A SURPRISE PARTY

SPOTLIGHTING

"PINK"

LEMONADE

Kathryn SchwauSch Branson
7-10-2025

RAT HOLE

Faith Has Proven Well

People can be cheerful, kind to you in public,
acting like you are an ideal, welcome friend,
forgetting that we live upon a fallen world.

Sooner or later their true selves break loose,
striking, biting you with poisonous juice;
coiling in circles like a snake wrapping itself
tightly about your neck to crush you down.

You are stumped, confused, as to how you
were so easily tricked and duped by a con.
The last and first thought in your mind is
why you chose to believe nonsensical lies,
causing ones you love to cringe and cry
after you have been so obviously fooled,
your mind unaware of humans being cruel.

Gossip, searing words aimed at your family;
the con man needles, forcing you to crawl.
You shrink, sliding in a rat hole on the wall.
Inside, you have evaporated, withered small.
You question whether to flee away but stall.

Living there, you grow strong and stand tall.
Now you are trapped and stuck deep inside.
The fact of squeezing yourself out means
ripping off most of your weathered hide.

You have an impossible decision to make:
you've no place to go, and no place to stay.
Still, there is always a duffel bag of choices.
Foes will chatter, blocking out God's voice.

He plans to take you along His secure way.
You see a tall, wide door He leads by pulling,
drawing you into an awe-inspiring,
most holier place.

Your Maker closely guides you safely there.
When you slip on a ledge, He halts your fall.
God's angels swing the gates wide open.

Entering in, you walk within Heaven's hall.
You step on gold, He beseeches you to stay.
His beloved Son for us He freely gave,
assuring you to never fear or scream in vain,
hearing no more raging, untruthful blames.

Believing, God has given you a purest name.
He chose you long before time ever came.
Leaving earth, kneeling down, arms abreast,
eternity is welcoming a child God claimed.

Harmonizing with His blessed,
your almighty Lord's
praises magnificent,
the first, not last.

He washed away all shame,
humbly proud the same.

Faith has proven well.

GOD'S PROMISE

HE WOULD

SAVE

Kathryn SchwauSch Branson
7-11-2025

RED WAGON

Little Red Wagon

Time carries age along,
with it right behind,
being pulled strong
inside our little red wagon,
where we hang on.

Our little red wagon
never grows up
or gets bigger—
it only gathers
dust and rust.
Age can't waver
her state of robust.

Red wagons come with time.
When young, we get in as we climb,
settling into a comfortable spot.
Age is a hussy hitchhiker,
unsolicited, unwelcome,
making us fidget;
we can't fight her.

We try to accept life's
rides and its curves,
avoiding the swerves.
We stay in our wagon
until God's appointment
comes to move us out.

Then other children are given
our little red wagon.
Angels lift us with wings;
flying up, we reach
heaven to sing.
Enraptured, we fling,
bidding earth farewell,
telling it to color us gone.

Goodbye, red wagon,
we must move on,
pull other children
until God's clock
rings His angels
to take them out.

While our little red wagon
on earth continues to roll,
it stays and refuses
to disappoint.
Little ones, so its
wheels never
stop.

Diligent and proud,
taking all of the children who
crowd into our beloved,
never forgotten,
little red wagon.

Kathryn SchwauSch Branson
7-27-2025

L.E.'S EYES COLOR BEYOND "ALWAYS"

Have you seen her face?!!!

No, not yet but her turning side view

Is a streak of light astounding Sunshine

Casually let through

Her poise is so unimposing

It imposes on you

Excited to meet her, up the hill

Walking with strained steps , I go

Then seeing her face shimmering

Sounded off a musical trill

It's framed in long strawberry blonde

Red hair splashed about her skin

Which is strong, sound, crystal clear

A delicate rose bud fair, frail, soft; thin

Saying hello, she smiles as if opening

A window into the future's weather

Predicting magnificent skies tucked

Amongst days void of pleasure

The moment they met

Two sparks collided

No doubt about it; a split second

Timeless abided

Which set off LOVE,

Caring and intimacy

Suffering in separate lapses

Tolerating some future to be

Unbearably harsh and frightfully

Broken by Longing

To lose it's way ; in confusion

When it COLLAPSES

Young love can be so intense

It reverses yourself out of you

Shaking strong it makes you reel

Shoving away GOD it stands rude

To our temporary "ALWAYS"

Its hope is to crush and steal

Placing OUR LORD underneath

Perfection is not ultimately achieved

Between The Ones our Lord Oversees

So if you feel you've met that Soul

Who you think has made you whole

GOD will forbid it

HE ALWAYS maintains control

Your being must stay in service

Unstopped by lovers that

Want to share You with HIM

So when someone disrupts your

World and essence within

Pushing apart your true bond

With GOD

HE who has begun it; has to

Stop it and say, "END"

In HIS compassion and understanding

HE will rain showers of LOVE MEMORIES

Which Divinely HE forbids to fade

Although poured from HIS HANDS

Being GOD; HE allows them to float

Being merciful HE will not let them Land

These chapters of our lives are like us

They are temporal and belong up above

Our most BEAUTIFUL feelings give us

A glimpse of our sacred marriage

To our LORD; the closet LOVE

We will ever have; it's a foretaste

Of "ALWAYS" STAYING SAME

So when we find ourselves lost

There's no need on this meager earth

To savor regret or moan loss

GOD'S CHOSEN ORDAINED CHILDREN

HE will not release or share with others

Time before "ALWAYS" was

"ALWAYS" with HIM

He allowed drifters in and out of our lives

Yet HIS love was forever folding

Caressing us within

GOD'S LOVE IS NO WHIM

If we glance back with sadness

Assuming we misplaced our "ALWAYS"

Greet your Holy Spirit with smiles

To HIS Eternal joy undying GLADNESS

Remembering those igniting sparks

Which flamed so bright on earth

Were only a light on earth's Heavenly

Domain we walked holding hands

Briefly here through HIS PARK

But upon exiting HIS GARDEN

The closing gate broke our HEARTS

Because every second in time

Is followed by another

"ALWAYS" isn't "ALWAYS"

Once gone; impossible to recover

GOD has HIS reasons

HE gives and HE takes

Promising all our Blessings

We thought lost will again bound

By Our Lord's Love inside GOD'S SAKE

When we enter HIS Mansions

HE SAYS HE WILL LEAD US AND

HIS TIMING IS PERFECT

HE MAKES NO MISTAKES

GOD'S creatures are adorned

In most splendorous colors

Then in a blink this fleeting hue

Intertwined between Lovers

Takes its place beneath GOD

We obey and choose the narrow gate

Walking HIS way which is very straight

If we tarry holding onto those "ALWAYS"

Making GOD wait; our lives might

Be ended; our Souls might terminate

In thinking we have found someone

Who ends our search on earth

Being GOD'S ordained and Chosen

Then this "someone" we must lurch

Our time with Birthdays

Proceeds forward to GOD days

Angels are waiting to lift us

Up in their softer than snow wings

When we enter the banquet; JESUS

Our Husband in Glory we TAKE

Treasures and moments we've

Gathered on our way

Will not be forgotten; although in

Living they flitter and scatter while

Falling down along GOD'S garden

They are "ALWAYS" saved by

The invisible One who creates Eyes

Vast beyond Color

These heartaches were Gifts HE gave

Waiting to be whole again repaired

In His Heavenly Home's care

Letting go of earth's "ALWAYS"

That abandoned us in despair

We rest assured in THE "ALWAYS"

OF ETERNAL LIFE AS

JESUS

WILL BE THERE

"JESUS CHRIST THE SAME

YESTERDAY

TODAY

AND FOREVER"

Giving us "ALWAYS" LOVE

WE WILL ON AND ON

SHARE

Kathryn SchwauSch Branson
1-10-2026

REINVENT YOURSELF

Take My Hand

Take my hand let's dig our toes

Curling them into the sand

Next to the agitating ocean waves

JUST LIKE WHEN

We did the times before my legs

WOULD NOT MEND

Stuck here now settled into faded blue

This can't be me tripping on my own shoe?

Barefoot works a little "IFFY" but safe to do

Life can get ruined when hate rams into you

THEN IT'S TIME TO

KEEP YOUR SPIRIT'S LOVE

TURN YOUR MIRRORS AROUND ANEW

Because the life you had has left; jilted you

Out of your reach your old path—up and flew

It tilted you off the shaky edge of a cliff

SPLAT INTO A BROKEN WATER SPEW

A GRAVE HIT

BACK UP – U – TURN – RENAVIGATE

CAST AWAY ALL GLOOMING HATE

REINVENT YOURSELF

OPEN UP OLD GATES

WALK ON IN

DON'T WAIT OR HESITATE

YOUR NEW LIFE BEGINS

A SMALL SHEER CIRCLE

Seek a drop of LIFE ferried deep that's true

Tie all loose strings into a perfect ball

Ignore the grey; paint your sky a royal blue

Broken pieces scattered all about

Your heart is churning; in need

OF GOD RETURNING

PUMPING BLOOD

ALIGNING YOU

HE HAS ON HAND

HIS MIRACULOUS CAN

FILLED WITH HIS UNFAILING

REALIGNMENT PLAN FOR YOU

GOD'S OWN BONDING

DIVINELY MADE FOR

GATHERING BITS

STOMPED ON THE GROUND

ADHERING YOU

ALL FIT BACK TOGETHER

WITH GOD'S

DIVINELY INTRICATE

CELESTIAL

SANGUINE

GIFT OF JESUS'

BLOOD

UNFLAGGING

"SUPER GLUE"

Kathryn SchwauSch Branson
5-29-2025

REMINISCING RESCUED FURRY "DAISY"

From the moment we wake until we
cry out our first breath of life,
we experience gain each day that
sometime or another on this earth
will all go away.

Birth is the beginning of
weeping, shedding tears.
Death is the beginning of
our heavenly life with
no sorrow or fears.

All great, wonderful gifts come from God.
Some are delicate, small;
some grandiose and tall.
Daisy was all.

Our family, our friends, and our
beloved pets,
within our lifetime we were blessed,
miraculously met.

Daisy was lost; she was
abandoned on a street,
a beautiful, playful,
snuggly creature
for us to meet.

As God put her in your path to save for you,
she was splashed in a color of
honeysuckle dew.

Somehow she melted into your lives;
she flowed with love and glancing
keen cat eyes.

We don't know what came first
her love for us or
ours for her.

Maybe we met in the middle,
our time spent together
so marvelously close,
a living being we watched run and play.
How can she be gone from our sight,
our touch, our fun, and our day?

Her place with us now
disappeared in haze;
our eyes, so blurry,
spill tears all day.

While we wait in foggy delusion,
the obscuration of Daisy's clear, full view
the loss of her remarkable furry bed,
time's comforting nearness has put
us in a state of free-fall confusion.
We go on living; our demeanor is blue.

We miss our Daisy; she misses us too.
God created these wonderful animals.
His goal for our lives is to rescue their
Love, then comes the awe-inspiring, lofty,
luminous, magnificent, marvelous,
monumental, splendid gift of opulence
we receive from God: the supreme,
uplifting life experience reaching deep,
personal, supernatural love for another
being, which He bestows in us bliss.

God is good. He gives, and He takes
Away but His giving of life on earth
is leading us to the ladder where He
takes and steps us up to our forever
home with our loved ones and pets.

No ending of time,
where we romp together in God's
love to joyously roam in our new
eternal home,
with Daisy we hold on.

Kathryn SchwauSch Branson
6-2-2025

ROLLER COASTER

Life Is an Emotional Roller Coaster Ride

Life is an emotional roller coaster ride.
About the time you're all the way up,
you're headed for a downhill slide.
Hold your breath try to stay alive.

If life was an amusement park,
a fun trip to see Disney World,
all these ups and downs we'd
expect and they'd merely be thrills.

But life is, for certain, genuinely real.
Some of it's painful, hard to do;
others are an easy breeze,
sadly, very few of these.

Then there come out smiles;
they rise up from our hearts.
We show our teeth in splendor,
until blunt-force trauma renders,

knocking us toothless, mouths pressed shut.
We've lost our freedom to laugh,
refraining ourselves half-mast,
something about us died.

The good nighttime stories lied.
We no longer fall asleep and dream
about the Tooth Fairy bringing to us
a special, hidden-beneath-pillow surprise.

Our mourning sheets soaked all soppy wet,
we went to sleep with wet eyes weeping.
The morning wakes us to loud greeting,
from grating words and jarring orders,

telling us to hurry, get up, and go.
We have to do what we are told,
not just the times we're young,
but lasting out until we're old.

There are those very light-felt spells;
life begins, emotional feelings swell.
These are times we want to keep,
we try to tuck them inside, deep.

We roll we spin the long night through
Morning light shines away the dew
This means happiness to peep
Our vision now clear
Hope does leap

On this day the MIRROW reflects new teeth
A SMILE comes to us from Somewhere
We want to know but we don't dare
Try finding out as that might scare

It into hiding a place unknown
We know it comes out on it's own
As it's something we cannot stow
Away and Keep and not let go

So life much an Emotional Roller Coaster
RIDE ; We climb the steep grade
Once on top : We Smile
When LOVE and LAUGHTER falls to the ground

Our focus is strange / a full blown STUPOR
This is when we realize life mixed us up
Hence it is full with FRILLS and BLOOPERS
Baring loss from trials and DESERTERS

We stay along side life we learn it's signs
At times eyes twinkle others we go blind
We stare out way into the UNKNOWN
We walk our lifetime by our own
We're made to walk not let go

Those we LOVE
We hold most dear
So unprepared for them
To yank our hands away from theirs

Forcing Interwoven Hearts apart
Suddenly we are left alone
Standing stupid here
Unloved we moan

We won't go or stand in line
For a Roller Coaster that has
Crashed over on its' laden side
Ups and downs with bolty lashes

This rickety looping of boards
Crushed upon a savage mound
Our bodies scattered off the ride
Loved ones looked for are not found

In our lives Loved ones will come
In our lives Loved ones shall go
The only Hand that we're told
Is GODS' reaching out to grip

Take a strong grasp of us
Redeeming our lives to
Bring us back Home
Let's walk away
We'll Hold

As PEACE inundates the twists and turns
Feelings blasted lastly calmed
To settle Celestial on us
Into GOLDEN CROWNS

Standing tall with
Smiles filling Souls
We'll never more fall
Wild wayward into holes

Safe in GODS' Commanding Touch
Conclusion and for Closure Down
We will surely end UP IN HEAVEN
SAVED RELIEVED
LOST SHEEP
OUR SHEPPARD :
GOD HAS
FOUND

Kathryn Schwausch Branson
5-15-2025

SAFE

When you wake are you glad

Or when you wake are you sad

When I wake I'm in gripping pain

That hits my perception; I'm MAD

It dawns on me momentarily

This pain means TODAYS' LIFE

Which steers me to ponder on my

LORD and SAVIOUR : JESUS CHRIST

The pain HE endured ; OBEYING HIS OWN

FATHERS' WILL

Was more BRUTAL , HATEFUL , INHUMAN ,

SHAMEFULLY DESERTED BY DISCIPLES

Then withering slumped down IN THE END

Clinging lost in a vacuum of LONELINESS

Taking HIS LAST BREATH

UNDER HIS OWN FATHERS' WILL

HE WAS FORSAKEN BY OUR SINLESS GOD

WHO TURNED HIS PRESENCE AWAY FROM

The searing , scorched , shambled worlds

AMASSING heap of sin

CRUCIFYING

JESUS' TAINTED BLOOD COVERED SKIN

GODS' OWNSELF IN HIS SON WHO HAD

SWEATED BLOOD WHILE PRAYING

PLEADING REMOVAL OF THIS BITTER CUP

But then totally surrendering to HIS

FATHERS' WILL , SACRIFYING HIS LIFE

FREELY GIVING HIMSELF UP

Rescuing us from our coffins REVIVED

BEATING DEATH , the GRAVE , SO ONE DAY

WE'LL ARISE and SURVIVE

LIVING BEYOND THE HOURGLASS SAND

WORKING and WORSHIPPING

OUR LOVING CREATOR

IN HIS HOLY LAND

Our knees meekly bowing to HIM
OUR GOD AND OUR SAVIOUR
WHO LOVED US WHEN
WE WERE STILL LADEN
COVERED IN SIN
MISSING THE MARK
ALWAYS
FALLING SHORT

We'll never understand the GRINDING
DEPTH it took to RANSOM OUR WIN
TO BRING US IN TO ETERNAL LIFE
WHERE WE COME FACE TO FACE
WITH OUR CREATOR
GASPING
SHAKING
ARRIVING GODS' PLACE
WE FALL TO OUR FACE

GLORIFYING GODS'

FAITHFULNESS

HIS ABOUNDING GRACE

WE MUST ATTEMPT TO TRULY
CONTEMPLATE
EVERLASTING LIFE

"SAFE"

Kathryn SchwauSch Branson
5-25-2025

SANDSTORM

LOOK WHAT THE DESERT SANDSTORM
BROUGHT ALONG WITH IT, A PUP, FOR
MATTHEW, MY NEPH;
A MYSTICAL BLESS

Matthew coaxes me to write and
Gives me fondest reasons to live.

I look forward to Matt telling me
To "NOT" talk; but to PLEASE
"Hear Him Out"! ! !

As he shares his Living
Testimonial Journey,
Clinging to my phone,
Which shoots over Atomic
Sparks for me to receive;
Melt in and join in his Reeling,
Swirling within Cushy Clouds—
His Tireless EFFERVESCENCE,
Raw Strength, and, I'd say,
"Right off my Cuff,"
His Indispensable HIGH,
Leaping Bounds; Blasting out,
Floating miles with both feet
WAY off the Ground!

Vigorously energized in his
Eternal Quest: a Search for
The GIST of all our Lives;
Where IT is taking us to,
Toward that On-Going,
Never flaming out-pilot:
BEACON; OUR LIGHT!

MATT is a man GOD'S SPIRIT
Contorted Perfectly,
Timing the Moment
Of most Dire Need,
Blending it in with
SmOOth HarmOny ♪♪♪

Our MAKER and GIVER,
In HIS OMNISCIENT TRACK,
Took HIS Valued CREATION—
MATTHEW'S SPIRITED.
- - Once TRAPPED - -

SOUL and BODY

FINALLY

FLYING :

ALAS ~~~

MATTS' "BEING"

" SET">>>

{{ FREE }}

✝

Kathryn SchwauSch Branson
5-30-2025

SAUCER EYES

After a lengthy time when consciousness
Had lapsed :: all of a sudden one morning
I ABRUPTLY WOKE UP,
        JUST LIKE THAT.

Momentary panic, because I had no earthly
Idea which place in the hospital I was in.
I turned to look toward my left, and in a
Chair was the reassuring sight of my Son
Sitting there, infusing me with life, revisiting
Myself; awake, reassessing.

Then swallowing, I asked the nurse what
Was all the glass in the back of my throat?
She said, "Be quiet. It was meant to be there."
Later I learned it was a feeding-tube snare,
A warp of plastic jabbing like porcupine hair.

Next thing I noticed were my wrists tied
Down by restraints hooked to the bed rail.
Politely I asked the nurse to untie please,
I was awake, and these were a grip, a TRAP.
Her answer, without looking, was a NO-WAY.
All the units I'd been in were an aura of SAME.

I decided if she didn't want to untie me well,
I'd just take care of it without help myself.
Yanking up my right hand with a forceful
Tug-of-war, I ripped that cuff into the air.
It was anchored about an A-line, not to pull
By me accidentally while in my dream world.

My eyes followed blood pumping out in a
Pattern round about a figure-eight lasso lair.
Then my eyes were drawn to my Son, who
Also stared while holding onto his chair,
Drawn to his eyes, looking round as saucers,
Reflecting messages of confusion and fear.

The nurse stood away, tapping frantically
On a computer screen; she must have
Been abhorred, asking why I was being ugly.
No doubt she was mean, but I kept on track,
Asking very politely to untie my left hand.
A second nurse, with big eyes too, quickly
Reached past my Son, cutting ties undone.

Not dawning on me, it was to save my IV.
The plan was to knock me out with drugs.
Last thing I saw before the lights went out
Was a vision of my Son's saucer-round eyes,
Beaming as we made a close eye-contact.
Austin's presence snugged me in comfort.

It edged in my Soul, his and God's devotion,
To not abandon me, by bringing my Son
To hang out in a hospital, even though his
Aversion to the sickness and smell in a
Fluorescent-lit maze of corridors next to
Rows of square confines

Blocking off patients alone
To heal themselves
Enduring through

TIME

Kathryn SchwauSch Branson
<date>

SING : BEAUTIFUL SAVIOUR
SCHÖNSTER HERR JESUS

The beauty of the day
No price tag nor display
The loveliness illuminates itself aglow
It marches on
Row by Row by Row

Entering the auditorium we feel no dread
Isle and number before HE has preset
Our place by HIM is Guaranteed
We need not circumvent our seat

It is complete with alphabet prior met
GOD'S gift to us through His own SON
JESUS CHRIST

My pride , my joy , my only ONE
I long to join the Lamb above
He is my cherished faithful Love

When I arrive I'll fall down on my knees
All the while my Soul will swell with pride
With blood stains showered over me
Shed on that dark momentous day
My Saviour hung and died

Upon a tree
To set me free
Bring me Home
Ransomed Redeemed

MY LIFE FREED EVERMORE
INTO ETERNAL

BLESSED JOY TO FEEL
DEEPLY CENTERED
WITHIN ME

.

Kathryn SchwauSch Branson
7-25-2025

SWEETPIE

Won't You Come Back

Loving me,

Thinking I am a person
To be proud of.

Whatever caused you to run
Away from Home,
What bandit came in and
Stole your Throne?

My heart's burdens are sinking down
Under the weight

Of not having your Confidence,
Your Caring,
Your Faith.

The sun is much dimmer,
Stars shine without luster,
The atmosphere is disappearing as
Grey fog has set in.

Bring back your HEART, my SWEETPIE.

Let's talk walking in the woods;
We won't need to say goodbye.
Tomorrows ahead are good,
For many hugs and waves,
Fingerprints on the windows,
Beating out sounding thoughts,
Caressing and sweet.

I love you, my Precious,
My only girl child elite.

You'll always be my SWEETPIE.
Until the day that I die,
You will remain my SWEETPIE,
Once we've reached His Sky.

Kathryn SchwauSch Branson
8-35-2025

THE BIG FISH

Who goes fishing by diving off the end
Of a very long Lake Geneva dock?

Believe it or not, my Son, Austin, did.
The cold water was a necessary shock.

It was a carefully planned, adventurous
DADDY /// SON DAY!!

It was Shane's turn for a special way of
Spending time with Dad, going someplace.

Austin reserved a valued ONE-ON-ONE
Date for a fishing trip with Shane, his Son.

Fishing rod and reel and all accessories
Were packed in the van for this day to be.

Father, thinking an ordinary fishing day,
These events, though, are never ordinary,
When, in a young child's spacious brain,
Any and every possible occurrence
Could occur within a second spent.

Learning to cast out is a thrill in itself;
A tug on your line is something else.

Then comes hesitation of what's next,
Dad is guiding step by step how to reel,
Intermittent handling with some flex,
Teaching his Son a fisherman's feel,
Father not wanting this fish to steal.

Suddenly the spell of suspense

Bounces high up into full view,
There's a fish on the hook, and it's blue!

Excitement escalates with the two,
A challenge,and that is for sure.
There's a flat fish jerking on the lure;
This requires a dire requirement,
For keeping this fish in air environment.

Dad makes certain, stepping back,
Giving all the glory to his Son
For this exhilarating fish to sack.

Austin keeps prodding Shane,
Telling him to reel and maintain,
"Back up some and bring it on in!"

Upon the dock, so it couldn't slip off,
Preventing its escaping swim.

Intently Shane eases it close up to him;
Father and Son are watching the fish,
Enthralled as it careens about the air.

Suddenly, within an instant, the Bluegill
Smacks Shane flat on the side of his face!
Without a moment's hesitation to make,
He reflexively tosses it all back in the lake.

What other choice was he to take?

Rod rapidly splashes down and sinks.
Dad instantly dives into the spot where
It all had been so quickly thrown out,

Going deep, flapping arms all about,
Hoping to retrieve the fishing gear.

Holding his breath the water isn't clear,
Dad keeps diving, grasping to seek
A rod and reel falling way underneath.

Fully dressed and still wearing shoes,
He keeps on feeling for a line or pole,
Something soggy found all the way down,
Laying there and stuck on the ground.

The fishing rod and reel he meant to save,
Grabbing his claim, an awesome catch,
Aiming toward the top, he must look brave.
Holding his breath any more now is grave.

As he surfaces, Shane is elated seeing Dad;
A fish was secondary to the Father he had.

Dad pulling himself and the fishing apparel
Back onto the dock heavy from peril.

Both guys were safe, with a fish on the line,
A great success on a most regular time.

Shane caught a Bluegill flat-pan fish;
Dad caught a rod and reel on this trip.

Dripping wet Dad and smiling Son, Shane,
Upon arriving home into the kitchen came.

Mom is waiting for a captured supper to fix;
Hannah smiles with her charming soft lips.

Without one word, she questions her man:
"What have you done now, my wild husband?"

Next she congratulates Shane on his fish;
Then, looking at Dad, she approves his lift.

Off the bottom of a lake, the catch he makes
Call it a wet and wild successful outing on
A Father/Son plain, normal day that spun
Into a kid's memory of a spell well done.

Anything is possible and remarkable too
When a Dad sets aside time with his child.

Going out for just a nonchalant day,
Creating a moment in time forever to stay,
Composed of a Son's walk down a dock
Over Lake Geneva, where the water is deep.

Casting his line out, feeling no fear or doubt
About a chain of events that all turned out:
Catching a fish by himself, unsuspecting,
A rude slap to his cheek and reacting
By casting his whole rod back in to sink!

Having a Dad who dove in, no time to think,
Recovering his catch and fish on the brink
Of a day just as simple as one might blink.

When time's set aside for ONE-ON-ONE FUN,
As a Father plans a fishing trip with his Son,
Which proves anything is possible
When GOD comes along
All Life's Adventures.

THE BIG FISH IS WON

Kathryn SchwauSch Branson
9-29-2025

THE END OF TIME

Sadness doesn't come with time,
Sadness comes with choice:
A person's frame of mind.

Pain doesn't come with harm,
Pain comes with life:
A baby being born.

Loneliness doesn't come with isolation,
Loneliness comes with:
A block of all relations.

Fear doesn't come with lack of courage,
Fear comes with:
A doubt of God's Marriage.

Death doesn't come with a last sigh,
Death comes with:
A passage to Eternal Life.

God has promised us Heavenly Mansions,

Without Sadness,
Without Pain,
Without Loneliness,
Without Fear.

THE END
Comes with:

THE END
OF TIME.

ENDING.

Kathryn SchwauSch Branson
7-27-2025

TINAS' TORMENTING TUNNEL

Breathing but NOT Breathing

TINA, you were gasping
With all your might—

Trying desperately to suck into your lungs
OXYGEN; but you failed and
Felt no air being allowed
To cross through a shield or enter inside.

A strangeness was blocking your lungs
From expanding,
As your Cardiomyopathy
Had caused a massive Pleural Effusion.

This liquid was filling,
Crushing your lungs down,
Making expansion an illusion.

While in the lab, getting a CAT scan,
You noticed the technician darting out,
Frantically going to get help fast.
You knew, that moment, you might not last.

Soon medical personnel entered the room,
Telling you little, with scurrying, swift moves.

You caught sight of a needle and syringe,
With alcohol swabs prepping your sides,
To insert a chest tube for fluid to slide.

You watched it flowing freely into a
Canister below, filling it up.
It drained, and it drained,
Two liters, it showed.

About this time, your BREATHING
Was "BREATHING"; but the danger
Was not over still, as another tube was
Placed in the other side of your chest.

You watched once again, fluid flowing
Quite fast into a second canister,
Collecting another full liter of fluid
That was still causing collapse of
The other lung, with fluid still in.

This was such a near-death experience
For Tina, her husband, and four children,
That finding the right words to explain
Falls short of the sinking feeling that
Comes when a person experiences
The absence of air; your heart racing,
Overworking for your very life to spare.

Your chest went hollow because a
Freight train tore clear through
Your aching Heart.
If it had not been
Hauling so many
Boxcars, the pain
May not have been
So unbearably hard.

The air blowing through this tunnel,
Collapsing lung with each heartbeat,
Would not feel so balmy, yelling defeat.
If only the burning smoke would blow
Away and leave; but this freight-liner's
Destination was scheduled to go NO WHERE.

And who knows how many
Miles are still left to this
Uncanny stop going straightly to Nowhere.

The map doesn't spot it, nor does
The latest GPS trace place.

It was in this state that Tina felt peace.
She surrendered herself to GOD,
Journeying between LIFE and DEATH,
Trusting HIM to make the best decision.

As Tina was suspended inside a tunnel,
Which would eventually shut down,
The only way possible to prevent
Was with The Good Lord's Hands
Wrapped completely around it,
While gently squeezing softly,
Hugging but being careful
So as not to rend.

Prayer will speed up the process.
The damage is too much to seal,
So patience and hope and belief
Are the most important and real
Ways to manage the time it takes
For your Heart, in God's Hands, to
Become healed and totally mend.

If only the boxcars would come to an end,
And the lighted bars would start to move
Up again; then your hands would be
Freed from ropes interwoven in knots,
Unraveled to let you grab hold of the
Steering apparatus that carried you
Lamentably through pain and dismay.

During your fast-beating heart, there also
Came a waving, pounding, terse headache.
Bound in dark quiet was all you could take.

Tina was facing the thought that this train,
Through the black tunnel, might never end.
She realized how much blood, sweat, and
Fears, along with GOD, Tina, and doctors,
It would take altogether, in order, plus more
FAITH in bringing the couplers close enough
To lap onto each other needing ALL
To be able to meet, locking it together.

A steady pace requiring extraordinary
Strength and flexibility to maintain
Unity over hills, curves, and rough terrain.

Thankfully, a Soul is remarkably shaped
In such a way that reflects GOD'S HANDS.
Tina then lifted the train, leaning over land;
Adrenaline flowed into Tina—clenching
The couplers in place, setting this derailed
Train back on its track for rolling to begin.

GOD is well aware you are just a woman,
Made and created by GOD from rib of man.
Tina, you are ambitious, efficient, family-
Oriented, while adoring your children
With a profound love for your Husband.
You struggled to keep going; now WEAK,
GOD was right there extending HIS ARM,
Taking over full control with His plan,
Which, to all who witnessed this event,
Seemed an impossible salvage to an end.

GOD wielded this chaos, complexing a way
Of leading this speed-demon, directing
It on a straight path above a deep canyon,
Approaching pointed rocks and razor-sharp
Blades, preventing any humanly way to

Slow down or divert the inevitable fall
Into a massive crash with a grinding,
Splitting sound of the entire Freight Train,
Hauling off all of your breathless pain.

The echo will resound across the canyon,
Reverberating miles stacked upon miles,
Causing an earthquake to bury the debris
That consisted of all you endured and
Lived, channeling across this dark tunnel.

Because of your good, solid Heart, GOD
Himself will grab you near, next to the edge.
He'll pull your Body high up to HIS CHEST.
Safely rescued, you feel
GRATEFULLY BLESSED.

Sitting COZY, SAFE, AND SOUND,
ALL MELLOW PEACE WITHIN FOUND,
YOU are wrapped IN GOD'S ARMS,

Settled on HIS LAP.

Your HOPE Restored,

GOD'S LOVE

SURELY

ABOUNDS.

Kathryn SchwauSch Branson
7-30-2025

TRUNKS

Shredded Paper,
Yellow Valentines,
Once a Hope Chest,
Red Love Letters,
Turned to Ropes,
Knurled in Twine.

TRUNKS.

Pictures of Two,
Homecoming Dances,
Framed for Keepsake,
Black Velvet Sashes
Aged with Holes,
Gone First Chances.

TRUNKS.

TRUNKS with Hats,
TRUNKS with Wraps,
TRUNKS with
RIBBONS, LACE, and SNAPS.

TRUNKS.

TRUNKS with LOVE,
TRUNKS with Scraps,
TRUNKS with All
MY YESTERDAY MAPS,

Of: PLACES TO GO,
PLACES WHERE BEEN,

Not really places,
Just

PEOPLE they're IN.

141 ૭

Kathryn SchwauSch Branson
5-24-2025

TWINE

Twisted Moments

Twisted Time

Twisted Love

Warped and knotted, worn-out
Twisted Twine.

No beauty in a rope that's frayed,
No loveliness in frazzled maze.
The touch is rough;
The silk is now a
Long lost day,
Remembered not,
Gone worthless ways.

The human life all
Comes to this:
Thank GOD, OUR LORD;
His Promise true to us.

He gives Eternal Bliss,
We don't deserve
The Grace He gives.

He will undo these scars
And pain.

My rope must hold;
He will regain.
I can't let go,
The fall is far.
I must hang tight.

This twisted, worn-out,
Frazzled TWINE
Will bring me up
TO
LOVE DIVINE.

Kathryn SchwauSch Branson
5-20-2025

UPTURNED SMILE

Jacquelyn's smile is an alluring model arch,
A symmetrical support of her radiant style.

Her days are filled with a reckoning force;
Some days go fast, others last a long while.
Like her smile, they curve upward, of course,
Connecting, blending high cheekbones,
Which transmit heat; her eyes open space,
Each segment pieced and perfectly placed.

When Jacquelyn looks down, one's first focus
Goes straight to her lips, lifting up motion
That crosses into a fleeting commotion.

Beneath her notable black riding hat,
She emulates striving and this surpasses
Any comprehension or understanding
From family, friends, or folks in rambling.

Lost to them is Jacquelyn's equestrian passion,
Her Dressage, built up over time
In dedication, with endurance evolving a
Continual flow of flawless progression,
That she's unable to link into their minds,
Preventing a grasp of the depth aligned,
Which came from arduous, cold winter days.

Creating a mysterious portrait of majestic
Performance deserving worldwide display,
Jacquelyn mastered this skill of combining a
Stately horse to mesh with its teacher's way,
Engaging to satisfy and please her will,
Unaware of exhaustion, without any praise.

Ambitious desire merged within yearning;
Each day was part of her story advancing,
A complex step penetrating, forwarding to
The time she would be competing, facing
A magnitude of spectators' keen-eyed view
Of judges interspersed, each rating every
Contestant's meticulous shape and move.

The moment this came to a serious climax,
This unity of a girl and her horse emerged,
Energized, scanning the crowd as they sat,
Expecting the embodiment of an elitist,
Competing and exhibiting a fine work of art.

Jacquelyn's turn came into play entering the arena,
Her upturned smile covertly hiding any sign
Of fear that might hint apprehension or delay.

This ominous sparring with masters began.

Jacquelyn became ONE with her beast as she
Appeared with her mount, prancing proudly
Praising his mentor, trained to feel her lead.

People in rows, staring, transformed into a
Hypnotic, spellbound state blocking speech,
As this girl embraces, liquefying with Horse.

Simultaneously, her stallion surrenders to
His Rider, creating an enthralling pattern,
Exhibiting a rhythmic slide embodying
An awestruck sight of synchronized motion,
Emitting dynamism hijacking the eyes of all
Who gaze upon this performance as
They no longer perceive sitting, but float
Out of their chairs while following the girl
On her gaited companion together in glide.

Yet in the corner of each spectator's eye
Comes a distinctive, unique, incomparable
Sight of lips shaped superbly, collecting
Equestrian essence while conveying why
JOY is spread around everyone's presence
Who captures JACQUELYN'S
"UPTURNED SMILE."

Kathryn SchwauSch Branson
5-21-2025

WHY THINGS

Why do women hit and
Slap faces of men?
Why do women argue
And holler at men?

"Why are these men,
The ones women know,
The ones who
Deeply love them?"

Why do women push
And shove men?
Why do women control
And own men?

"Why are these men,
The ones women know,
The ones who
Deeply love them?"

Why do women take
Friends from men?
Why do women take
Away family from men?

"Why are these men,
The ones women know,
The ones who
Deeply love them?"

Why do women tell lies
And distort men?
Why do women hurt
And harm men?

"Why are these men,
The ones women know,
The ones who
Deeply love them?"

Why do these women start out by
Loving these men?
Why do these men start out by
Loving these women?

The love came first;
The war came later.
It's been said that the
Answer to these whys
Boils down justly to
An old, parted lore:

"All is fair in love and war."

I want to declare there's no
Such thing as we all know,
There are war crimes committed;
Fair isn't in them,
As pain's not omitted.
Fair is merely lost and not found
In love and war.

Where lives the answer to these
WHY THINGS?

Men will go on forever
Loving beautiful, sexy,
Flirtatious, alluring,
Seductive, charming,
Attractive, captivating,
Sometimes accidentally
Coy, crazy women.

AND ALSO, LIKEWISE:

Why do men hit and slap faces of women?
The story's the same;
The ending's no different.
It all traces back to a handed-down lore.

" ALL IS FAIR IN LOVE AND WAR "

Kathryn SchwauSch Branson
7-27-2025

CLEVER POWER

I remember forlorn, riding my horse Molly,
Down the cow path into the pasture high
Looking out across the far, settling sky,
Wondering if I'd ever have someone who
Was standing close by, singing songs of
Love while looking sweetly into my eyes.

With a force of soaring words unsaid,
Only whispered softly to me in his bed.

This span of youth held me thinking I am
Not all I need, but someone else can give
To me the rest of what it was for me to live.

Knowing more would be required to fill this
Void I felt inside, staring into a vacant and
Disappearing, vastly fading, vanishing sky.

What makes a person yearn for another,
Just to find out in the end they can never
Quite cover any of the emptiness, the lost
Sense of self or even be a faithful lover?

This is a fragile span in life, between the day
Of having home and the day of going away,
To live somewhere strange and be all alone,
With the complete unknown of how to cope.

Catching sight of a sexy guy walking by,
But feeling apprehension, looking down shy.
Inside you, his mystic way caught your sight,
Looking ambitiously smart, not noticing me.

Then the time came he asked you to go out,
In your wildest mind's eye, this was a dream.

Then when he did, you learned he was a
Sinking hole hearing his search in life was
Centered on being hooked on drugs and
Casual, freelance sex with girls who'd join
Him in moving to California, where they are
Easy to buy or find—fulfilling a wish, wasting
Your time standing still, flying high, merely
Living a way to grow old, aging weirdly.

There is a feeling buried somewhere inside,
Craving a cure to release you from a trap.
Of feeling needy for a man who gives you pride
From the impact he has on you in one look.

Then your heart is smitten by a sharp hook;
He reels you in fast, you belong to him soon.

You think surely when you give love out,
It will return also back to you somehow.
This is just a simple myth, as a gift is a gift.

Once you give of yourself, you lose that bit
Of who you are as a man takes you, in a split
Second holding you, until he leaves to quit.

You're once again staring into a vanishing
Sky you remember from years ago grieving,
Sitting on your horse, feeling a vacant heart,
Asking yourself and still wondering WHY.

Loving someone so much
Has the clever power
To make you
CRY.

Kathryn Schwausch Branson
7-26-2025

WORLD WAR'S END

If you think that the devil is going to
Leave YOU alone.

YOU'RE
DEAD
WRONG.

That's his very first sign
You've just let him in.

He Gloats
His WIN.

Is there a Soul on the Earth
The devil's not out to get?

NO,
NOT EVEN
ONE.

Lucifer was cast out of HEAVEN;
He was given ALL EARTH to ROAM.

OPPOSING GOD IS
satans'
HELL -BENT- GOAL.

Between GOD and the devil, a DO-OR-
DEATH WAR BECAME,

THE WORLD'S
MOST COSTLY
COMBAT FOR FAME.

GOD SAYS "I AM"; devil said, "we'll duel,"
Coveting GOD'S CREATION,
Man made in HIS IMAGE,

CLAIMING AS CHILDREN,
CHRISTENING WITH SOULS.

Lucifer BEFORE SHONE, BEAMING A GLOW;
Now he was dropped second-hand to man.

His evil more powerful still
Though than earthlings,
He destines to kill.

Not willing to be submissive or obedient to
The ONE TRUE TRIUNE WHOLE,

He BECAME ENRAGED
When he was DISROBED.

In HEAVEN the devil was ENTICING,
BEING the BRIGHTEST ANGEL.

ONE THIRD OF THE
ANGELS BELOW HIM
He STOLE.

They were enamored with satans'
DEVIOUS PLAN to STEAL MAN'S SOULS,
Their new hero: RAMPAGING, BOLD,
To SUCCEED and HOLD

GOD'S CHILDREN DOWN
BELOW.

So ask yourself the main question,
If YOU FEEL YOURSELF FREED.

The answer is: YES,
JESUS DIED,
BUT HE ROSE AGAIN
ON DAY THREE.

However, the WAR, an ARDENT POWER
STRUGGLE of VIOLENCE for YOU and ME,
Our FOOTAGE on EARTH, we must keep our
EYES TURNED UP
TOWARD THE LORD,

WATCHING
HIS RETURN

ON THE LAST DAY.

TRUMPETS ANNOUNCING,
WITHIN GLORIOUS FLAMES
SURROUNDING JESUS COMING DOWN.

HIS FOLLOWERS TO LIFT UP
INTO HEAVEN'S HOME,
PREPARED FOR HIS SAINTS.

OUR MAKER'S PERPETUAL PROMISE,
PLANNED FOR HIS LOYAL CREATED ONES,
IN HIS OWN IMAGE, FORMED FROM CLAY,
TO FAITHFULLY FROM ALL WARS TAKE,

FOREVER PRAISING AND BOWING
ON OUR KNEES.

FOR GODS'

SAKE 🎁

Kathryn SchwauSch Branson
5-24-2025

PROSPERITY

It is so hard to stop roller skating

In a figure eight,
Marked with colorful chalk on a
Large concrete porch,
Built, giving kids a place to skate.

For once you begin, you pick up the spin;
While whizzing about, you focus to
Meet every mark, curve, twist, and turn.

Concentration and movement lull you,
A rhyming glide, mastering each swerve,
Skating without time interfering.

Open windows light this large figure eight;
Slowly dimmed sunlight allowing a place
For Mr. Moon marching on up to the stars,
Right adrift the entire Milky Way Galaxy.
Rolling by each window, a sight to see.

Suddenly you hear Mother calling:
"Stop now! Supper is ready time to eat."

You are held in a continuum of spiraling;
Once again you hear Mother calling,
"Hurry up, don't make me wait.
Food is on the table, getting cold;
You have your designated chair and plate."

At what point, though flowing along this
Fading, colorful figure-eight chalk drawn,
Does one decipher the ending spot is on?

You must simply grab tight of motion,
Rein it to cease while you try to retreat.

You hear Mother calling, "Come now!"

Then in the very middle crisscross of the
Figure eight, you abruptly stop to sit down
On the cool concrete floor; you hurriedly
Unlock your skates and free up your feet.

While walking inside, slow motion, you feel
Your eyes are still drifting as you say
Hello to night and goodbye to this day.

After supper and bath, you wiggle in bed,
Knowing when you wake up it will be
Play time again, as the windows welcome
The earth with bright sunshine to see.

During your slumber of night's evening,
Your dreams stay in motion with infinity,

Promising Life to

Continue

Coming

Going

Turning

WORLD WITHOUT END.

While wearing this nature & temperament

Continue to pass on and out-and-out
Spinning like a top hat
Twist our fate.

Kathryn SchwauSch Branson
August 8th,2025

AUSTIN'S HANNAH

Once I hurt a very Delicate Soul
At the time I was mistaken within
shallow thinking; that she was hurting me.
It's just that I was trivial and had
no clue as to the depth of her inner FEELINGS.

She seemed in "appearance" to be
offended by me in "my" home.
I was rude because of her angst
and uncomfortableness: her
TENDERNESS.

I HURT HER MORE THAN I DARE TO OWN.

My sorrow is deep for my undeniable
SIN. Her fragile nature was
weeping within.
She is not a "quick study," and one must
take their time in allowing this
exquisite creature to slowly
bring to LIGHT, in her own time
and how, she will unveil her
INTRICATE NATURE.

Hannah is a phenomenon, a marvel,
a sensation: a person turned
quietly in; for reasons belonging only
to the nature of her elusive character,
HER SOFTEST WHIM.

My harsh behavior "turned" this special
visit from my son and his "lovely"
pregnant wife into a topsy-turvy,

misconstrued jutting out of MY "chin."
My son was incredible; promising me
that our time together could
STILL BE A WIN.

If I would stop myself from this destructive
WHIRL-WIND.
I felt I had messed up too bad to do that;
but he said, "I could always change out my HAT,"
thus turning a one-sided spat into a dual,
God-momentous triumph and start of
LOVINGNESS FUEL.
Hannah wrote me a praising letter
I certainly did in no way deserve.
I'll keep it forever because it
truly, remarkably reveals
WHOM she serves: her LORD, who
created this fine-textured workmanship,
an enigma; belonging entirely to HIM.

It doesn't matter how low I feel about me,
God is forever forgiving; and this poem is
Wholly dedicated to a velvety flower with
ENORMOUS BLUE EYES, that most are unable to take in their
surrounding vision
In such an astounding magnificence as
Their eyes are no match for the range
HANNAH'S EYES GET

Because hers magnify GOD'S LIGHT
With an imperceptible SIGHT †

I ask you not to be duped by this
Diminutive girl's size or her beauty.
Although she is sensitive,
INSIDE she secures a secret TOWER

OF strength and wisdom
As she travels alongside GOD'S
Ascending pathway; gathering up
Knowledge and servitude and might.

Most of the time she is quiet and meek;
Lamentably, that's all you see if you
Unconcernedly only take a peek.
However, if you are attuned and intrigued,
You will push yourself to seek what's
Beneath her smooth, satiny, flawless
Skin; and then you might find a
Larger-than-life image fluttering
About and amongst ANGELS in our LORD'S
Heavenly, earthly
LAND.

Kathryn SchwauSch Branson
4-29-2025

EVAN WAYNE'S OWN EYEBALLS

I see your Brother!!! I SEE HIM 👀

He is behind you; hugging you

I see him - I Can See Him - I'M SEEING

You don't understand!!!!!! I AM

LOOKING AT HIM WITH MY OWN

EYEBALLS ◎◎

HE IS BEHIND YOU

YES, I BELIEVE YOU; I FEEL HIM

He did not fall

Evan Wayne and I knew he'd come

Behind me HE STANDS TALL

He has come to visit

He has come to comfort

He has come to SAY

My loved ones can COUNT on me

MY LOVED ONES I'll HUG

At times I come to lift up US

BECAUSE

I AM

YOUR UNCLE

""RUSSELL""

Kathryn SchwauSch Branson
1-10-2026

HOME

For the ones who can't see
The burning pain that angers me,
Blaming my wounded frustration on ADHD,
CUTTING ME OFF WITH YOUR
DEAFNESS BLOCKS ALL OF
MY SCREAMS.

For the ones who can't see,
Try on my shoes and follow me,
Step for step into deep holes I've
FALLEN IN.
ATTEMPT TO BEAT MY RAGING SOUL AND
SEE IF YOU WIN.

For the ones who can't see,
Pretend you are a CAT with NIGHT EYES.
YOU MIGHT BE SHOCKED,
WATCHING ME WRITHING ABOUT,
MY SLEEP WRUNG OUT,
TROUBLING PROBLEMS
YOU DON'T WANT TO SEE.
OR ARE YOU ONE OF THE ONES

Who can't see,
Who do not feel,
Who walk right through me,
Just as though I were a GHOST
PASSING AWAY, NOT TOUCHING
ME AS YOU GO,
THINKING MY VALUE IS
ONLY FOOLS' GOLD.

HAVE YOU BECOME ONE OF THE ONES,
MISSING SIGHT OF YOUR SON?

BEING YOUR CHILD, SHOULDN'T
"I" BE THE ONE
YOU SACRIFICE MOST OF YOURSELF,
IN LEADING ME ON,
HELPING ME FACE LIFE,
YOUR LOVE GIVEN ME FREELY,
EASING MY STRIFE?

OR ARE YOU ONE OF THE ONES
WHO NEVER SHEDS TEARS
TO WASH THE SMUDGE OFF
YOUR EYES, BLOCKING ANY
CLEAR, CLEAN VISION?

Maybe drawing this CAT
Would open others' eyes to the fact,
A LITTLE ONE'S LIFE DISMANTLED SURVIVING THE TEMPEST
HAS TAKEN
ITS TOLL ON
HIS WEATHERED BACK ALL THE DRASTIC DEBRIS
SCATTERED
INSIDE AND OUT HAS LEFT
A LONE CHILD ROAMING ABOUT
TO FIND HIS OLD smile
HIDDEN IN THE MAZE
HOPING SOME DAY TO
RECOVER AT LAST
HIS FORGOTTEN
CRYING
LONELY LOST
DROWNING
"laugh."

Kathryn SchwauSch Branson
6-9-2025

"FOR THE ONES WHO CAN'T SEE"

For the ones who can't see,
They're not blind,
They refuse to look
OR LISTEN,
NOT WILLING TO
FEEL.

For the ones who can't see,
They were blind when born,
GROPING DETERMINATION,
HOLDING A WISH TO
PERCEIVE,
RIPPLED WAVES OF VISION,
LATCHING WITH LONGING,
ACHING TO SEE.

For the ones who can't see
Into someone else's heart's held thoughts,
Wearing thick sunglasses, their insight is so
Dark; wincing when lights turn on bright,
ALLOWING OMINOUS
SHADOWS THAT
LURK WHILE TRYING
TO LOCK ME OUT,
STUCK IN YOUR RUT,
YOU CAN'T HEAR MY
SHOUT.

For the ones who can't see
How much their words are killing me.
Sticks and stones, I've had broken bones,
But the lies that were thrown
ABANDONED ME FROM
MY FIRST CHILDHOOD HOME.

Kathryn SchwauSch Branson
10-30-2025

GROUND ZERO

A story composed and recited to
His Grandma Branson
On 6-6-2025

"GROUND ZERO"

What some people say is that when you
die, you start at "Ground Zero."

But some people think and know,
that you don't start at "Ground Zero."

You start at GROUND ONE.

And you don't think it's a big feat;
but it's far larger than you've
ever started.

You walk through this place
that you have now entered;
and the streets are GOLD.

You wonder what this place is…
but you don't know.

BUT

you are NOT at

"GROUND

ZERO."

Evan Wayne Stansell's Story videoed
And put in exact wording
By Kathryn SchwauSch Branson on
10-27-2025

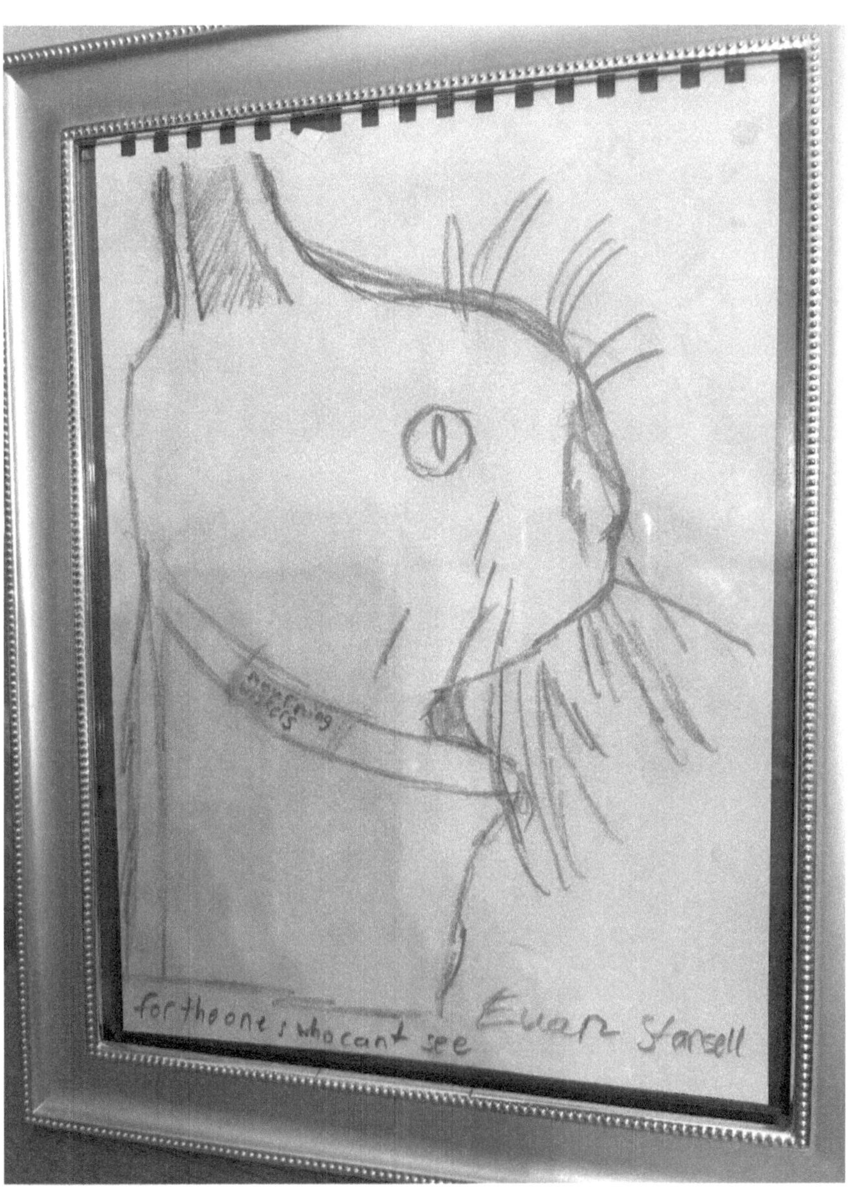

barking
orders
for the one s who can't see
Euan Stansell

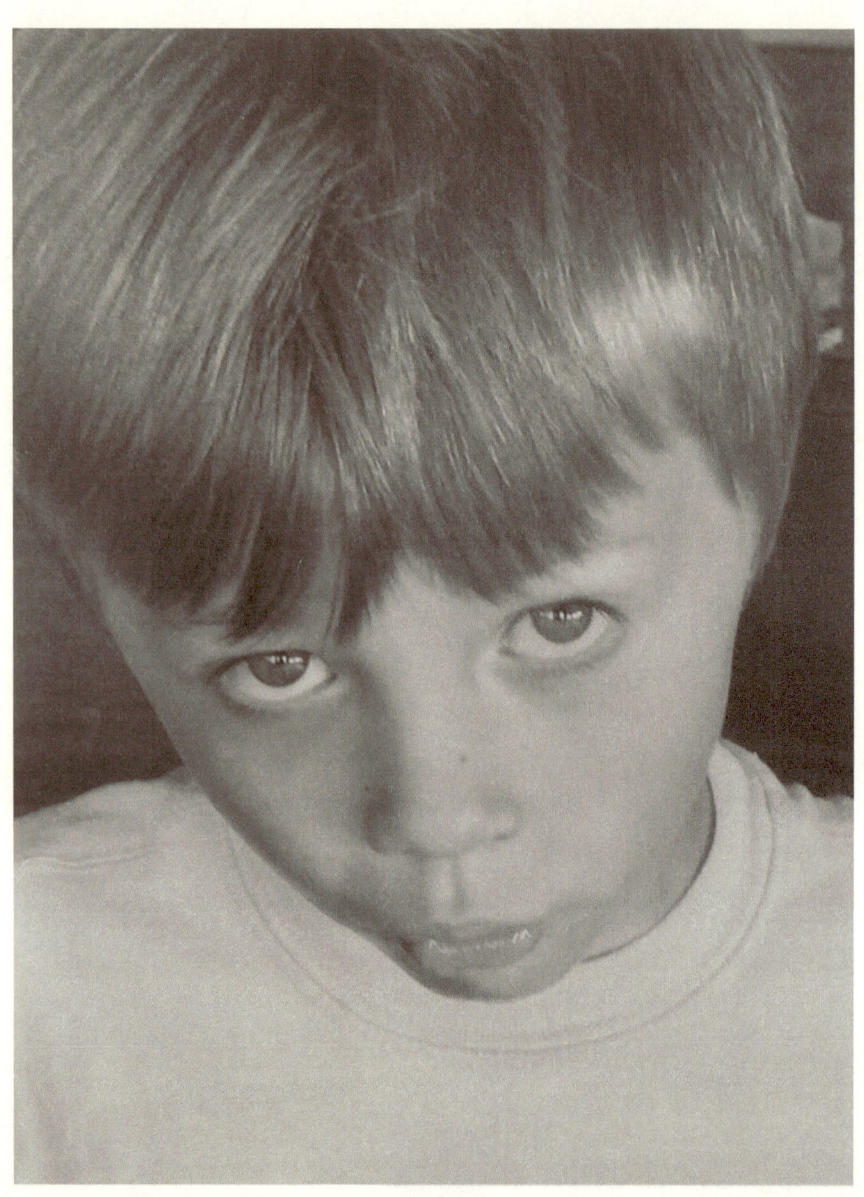